NEITHER KING NOR PRELATE

NEITHER KING NOR PRELATE

Religion and the New Nation
1776-1826

by
EDWIN S. GAUSTAD

WILLIAM B. EERDMANS PUBLISHING COMPANY
GRAND RAPIDS, MICHIGAN

Copyright © 1993 by Wm. B. Eerdmans Publishing Co.
255 Jefferson Ave. SE, Grand Rapids, Michigan 49503

First published 1987 as
FAITH OF OUR FATHERS: RELIGION AND THE NEW NATION
by Harper & Row, San Francisco.
This revised and corrected edition first published 1993.

Library of Congress Cataloging-in-Publication Data

Gaustad, Edwin S. (Edwin Scott)
Neither king nor prelate : religion and the new nation,
1776-1826 / Edwin S. Gaustad. — Rev. and corr. ed.
p.   cm.
Rev. ed. of: Faith of our fathers. 1st ed. c1987.
Includes bibliographical references and index.
ISBN 0-8028-0701-1 (pbk.)
1. Church and state—United States—History—18th century.
2. Church and state—United States—History—19th century.
3. United States—Church history—18th century.
4. United States—Church history—19th century.
I. Gaustad, Edwin S. (Edwin Scott)
Faith of our fathers. II. Title.
BR516.G36   1993

322'.1'0973 — dc20   93-35446
                                                    CIP

Cover art: John Adams, by Charles Willson Peale, courtesy of Independence National Historical Park; Benjamin Franklin, by Charles Willson Peale (after Martin), courtesy of American Philosophical Society; Thomas Jefferson, by Rembrandt Peale, oil on canvas, 1805, 1876.306, collection of The New York Historical Society, New York, New York; James Madison, by Charles Willson Peale, courtesy of The Thomas Gilcrease Institute of American History and Art, Tulsa, Oklahoma; George Washington, by Charles Willson Peale, courtesy of National Portrait Gallery, Smithsonian Institution, Washington, D.C.; Congregational Church, Newport, New Hampshire, courtesy of the Billy Graham Center Museum, Wheaton, Illinois.

For friends:

Robert T. Handy
Winthrop S. Hudson

Contents

LIST OF ILLUSTRATIONS

Acknowledgments

The origins of this book lie in the invitation of Union Theological Seminary (Richmond, Virginia) to deliver the Sprunt Lectures in 1986. I wish to express great appreciation to President T. Hartley Hall IV and his entire staff for their courtesy and gracious warmth during my week at Union. The church history faculty in particular extended every assistance, and my thanks to them are profound: James H. Smylie, Henry M. Goodpasture, and Rebecca H. Weaver.

Since that time, the lectures have been much revised and a new framework has been provided. Some material has appeared in altered form in Merrill Peterson, ed., *Thomas Jefferson: A Reference Biography* (Scribner's, 1986); and in Merrill Peterson and Robert Vaughan, eds., *The Virginia Statute for Religious Freedom* (Cambridge University Press, 1987). I express appreciation to both publishers for their kind permission to include here portions of materials under their copyright. I also thank two former students, Laurie Baker and James German, for their invaluable research assistance. Gratitude likewise is due those museums who gave permission. And, finally, my warmest appreciation to Charles Van Hof of William B. Eerdmans Publishing Company for his unfailing encouragement and support.

EDWIN S. GAUSTAD

1. An Introduction

As America approaches a new millennium, the religious arena is noisier and more crowded than many would expect. Newspaper headlines assault us, while bumper stickers insult us. Supreme Court decisions tumble over each other with a pace that is dizzying and with an array of opinions that is confusing. Strident slogans threaten civil discourse, and the church-state arena exudes the acrid smoke of battle: Prayer in the Public Schools; Tax Credits for Parochial Schools; Right to Life; Freedom of Choice; Absolute Wall of Separation; America as a Christian Nation; Intentions of the Founders; Creationism In and Darwinism Out. And so the cases multiply with attention to Sunday laws and flag salutes, voucher plans and baccalaureate services, nativity scenes and legislative chaplains. Anxious citizens might well ask, "Where will all this end?" And some of those citizens, in a nostalgic glance toward the past, may long for those idealized "good old days" when life was simple and all were agreed on basic values and basic beliefs.

One consequence of living in and reflecting only upon the ever-present present is that we are paralyzed by its complexity and confusion, its bewildering assemblage of options and decisions. We long for simpler times and calmer days, such a wish fathering the thought, if not the ironclad conviction, that those earlier days must have been simpler than our own, that options must have been fewer, and the paths ultimately chosen so much clearer. This is only another of the many ways in which we distort or trivialize the past, making it easier for us to misunderstand and more excusable for us to ignore.

The half century between the Declaration of Independence in 1776 and the deaths of Thomas Jefferson and John Adams in 1826 were years of momentous option and crucial decision. The years were neither simple nor calm, the paths chosen neither obvious nor inevitable. A Revolution fought and won, a loose Confederation transformed into a national Union, a West of unimaginable expanse claimed and won, a weak and vulnerable nation waging yet another war and fending off the threat of others—these events among many more point to the incontrovertible turbulence of these five decades. Though one may be ready to concede that, politically, these times did try the soul, it might nonetheless be argued that at least in the realm of religion life was far simpler then than now, decision making far less agonized and options far more restricted. After all, the argument might go, our ancestors did not confront secular humanism or aggressive Hinduism or flagrant pluralism. Protestantism prevailed, with the great Catholic and Jewish immigrations yet to come. The "good old days" must have been good in at least this respect: that the widest religious option presented to the American public in those years was merely the choice between being a Presbyterian or a Baptist.

And so we trivialize our own history, explaining to ourselves how heavy is our burden, how enormous our challenge, how perplexing our navigational task in charting the course ahead. The chapters that follow in this book should disabuse us of any notions of simplicity or ease even in the religious arena. Far more of the nation's future was shaped in this half century than can ever be suggested by the Presbyterian/Baptist option or any other comparable alternative. Nor does it make sense to discount the weight of religious options by citing meaningless statistics on church membership in this period: meaningless because no one knows just what the figures were, and because church membership was not then a perfect measure (if it ever is) of religious interest and influence. In so much of the colonial period, the problem was how to get onto a church's rolls, in contrast to more modern periods when the problem has been how to get off those rolls. Just because religion was taken so seriously in the earlier period, membership was neither lightly granted nor lightly received.

The questions raised in this half century, however, pushed far beyond that of who belonged to or attended church and who did not. The place of the Church itself in society, and especially with respect to political authority, occupied many a page of print and raised many a zealous passion. And well beyond the Church itself, what of the religious spirit or the religious life? Was religion essentially private and individual, or was it inescapably public and corporate? What was the relationship between religion and morality: entirely separate, mutually interdependent, wholly identical? Did theological conviction depend chiefly on reason, or revelation, or experience, or custom? Was diversity in denominational life a good thing or a bad, and did the surface variety conceal a more fundamental unity? And then the inescapable fact of a new nation facing a suspicious if not hostile world, facing a beckoning or barbaric wilderness, facing issues of divided sovereignty and unsettled loyalty—what was its peculiar responsibility or challenge with respect to religion? Two hundred years under the Constitution has given today's American public at least a frame within which to raise and offer responses to these questions, but in 1776 no such frame existed. The future was as uncharted as the trans-Mississippi West and the options as limitless as the cosmos. In the beginning was complexity, and the complexity has endured.

In order to appreciate the choices then, and perhaps to inform the choices now, it may be useful to delineate seven varying perspectives that guided or inspired men and women in our half century. These perspectives were not necessarily contradictories, though often they were contraries. Some could be held together in creative tension; others were seen as absolute dichotomies, either/ors that allowed no fence-straddling or ambiguous compromising. All required decision and judgment and conviction, as Americans in this time sought to shape and affirm that which would set the terms of religious life for centuries to come. This was accomplished, remarkably, without wars of religion, without a Tower of London or gallows or a guillotine. It was not accomplished, however, without controversy and discord and deep division of opinion. Civil discourse nonetheless continued, as indeed it must even centuries after.

ESTABLISHMENT AND SOCIAL ORDER.

The majority of citizens in the Western world, especially those in positions of authority, read their history as evidence, overwhelming evidence, that religion had a prime obligation, in partnership with the state, to preserve the delicate social fabric from disintegration or destruction. For the purposes of creation, God found it necessary to bring order out of chaos, and ever since, God's people have been charged with a similar task: to rescue humanity from its natural brutishness and anarchical selfishness so that a true society can be both formed and maintained. No Holy Roman Empire without a Holy Roman church, no English king without an English bishop, no German prince without a uniformity of religion in his region, no Mother Russia without a structured Orthodoxy directed from the "third Rome." If history proved anything at all, persons of this perspective argued, it proved beyond doubt that no state survived without its ecclesiastical alliance, and no religion deserved to survive that did not fulfill this essential societal function. And in making this case, the argument from "negative instances" was peculiarly potent: show us when and where in history the contrary has been true.

America was peopled by those familiar with this long historical experience, though a few sought escape from it. The vast majority, however, did not question the wisdom of the ages, the power of precedent, the inescapable logic that welded civil and ecclesiastical authority into a league powerful enough to exercise effective authority and cement social unity. When in the era of the American Revolution, John Adams faced a challenge concerning this perspective, which prevailed in Massachusetts, the wise statesman urged protesters to turn their attention and their energy toward more promising targets. Establishment of religion in Massachusetts, he assured his listeners, would endure as long as the solar system. That Adams's prophecy missed its mark by so wide a margin is not as significant as the assurance with which it was delivered and, by so many, received. Chapter 2 explicates the nature and extent of an assumption so deeply rooted in Western history, so firmly fixed in the collective mentality.

DISSENT AND PERSONAL PIETY.

Like a muted counterpoint, the dissenting tradition contested against that majoritarian view of religion and its societal priorities. Religion, in this perspective, had much more to do with the human heart than with the councils of state. Its essential nature resided in the deep reaches of human experience, the private recesses of encounters with the Almighty, the spiritual struggles and possible epiphanies. Experience preceded institution, not merely in obvious chronology, but in hierarchy of value as well. Institutions might come and go, might compromise and corrupt, might shatter and be reborn, but beyond and above all that was what God had written on the fleshly tablets of the heart. Though the voice of dissent was a minority one, it was far from a negligible one. Its history in England had been powerful in the seventeenth century and, sublimated into politics, continued its power in the eighteenth.

In colonial America dissent, with few exceptions, remained muted in the seventeenth century, but it erupted broadly and disturbingly thereafter. Especially in the wake of powerful preaching and anxious soul-searching in the 1740s and beyond, piety proved to be stronger than social order, careless of tradition, and impatient with the cold and formal institution. The Great Awakening, or the several sporadic awakenings, moved dissent from those deep recesses of the heart into the marketplaces and town halls, onto the agenda of both churches and legislatures. An itinerant ministry challenged the parish structure that prevailed from Virginia to Massachusetts; an evangelistic "born again" clergy found fault with ecclesiastical authority that preserved tradition but forfeited searing conviction. In the middle of the eighteenth century, this dissenting tradition shook the idea of an established church everywhere; it could not of itself turn the world upside down, but a generation later it helped others to do precisely that.

LIBERTY, CIVIL AND ECCLESIASTICAL.

A Declaration of Independence called for both liberty and life, a conjunction divine in its origin and inseparable in its nature, as

Jefferson had asserted earlier. In the midst of Revolution, many Americans found another conjunction never to be forced apart: political liberty and religious liberty. Just as civil and ecclesiastical tyranny had marched side by side through the centuries, each reinforcing the other and thereby swelling the flow of blood, so the battle for liberty could not cease until completed on both political and religious fronts. Americans resisted and feared and, at last, fought against the imperious overlords of England, and whether those overlords called themselves nobles or bishops or parliamentary potentates mattered not at all. If the power was imperious, as so often in the memories of the colonists it had been, then it must not be acceded to, under whatever pretense it came or whatever insignia it wore.

But even as independence from British authority was being won, anxiety about American authority arose. The capital defect of foreign tyranny was not that it was foreign, but that it was tyranny. So the Articles of Confederation represented the first timid steps toward an amalgamation that would allow some exercise of power—but not much. On the religious side, states moved quickly to curtail English ecclesiastical power but less decisively to nullify all politically aided churchly power. All disclaimed interest in religious persecution; all affirmed the benefits of toleration. Apart from this unanimity, however, one found in the revolutionary era and well after much uncertainty about the limits or implications of full religious liberty. Some wanted only so much liberty as was conducive to social order; others wanted only so much liberty as was supportive of Protestantism or of Christianity. Still others proclaimed liberty in stentorian tones only to reveal in concomitant actions that they hardly understood the central terms. Some worried that the state might be hobbled or hypnotized by the church; others worried that the church might be corrupted or seduced by the allurements of civil power. Thirteen separate colonies, lightly joined as confederated states, came close to having at least thirteen different opinions as to the true dimensions and proper directions of religious liberty. Chapter 3 features the two men who wrestled longest and most earnestly with this issue; they also happen to be the two men who gave sharpest definition to the argument and firmest direction to its future.

CIVIL RELIGION AND NATIONAL UNITY.

In some respects, this perspective on religion and its priorities is only another version of the first one, which honored establishment and social order. Here, however, one is not arguing on a theoretical basis about what religion by its very nature is charged to do. On the contrary, one in this instance is plunged into the midst of history, history of a particular people with a particular political destiny. That particularity had its archetype in the chosen Israel of old, a nation that was also a religious community. Both were sustained by divine power, both were under divine judgment, both represented "my people who are called by my name." And if such a nation/church transgressed, then it had God's promise that upon repentance the Almighty would hear from heaven, forgive their collective sin, and heal their land. That ancient promise had often been explicitly claimed by other nations in other lands in the name of other churches.

More often, however, the claims were implicit as one searched for that religious ingredient that somehow defined a people and gave them purpose. In the Western world biblical allusions and precedents have proved most compelling, since, for so much of that world's history, the Bible provided a common core of ethical teaching, of cosmic orientation, of historical unfolding, of metaphysical or theological underpinning. For Americans, too, the Bible supplied a unity that preceded and perhaps undergirded the political unity that was to come. The question was whether a new nation, not wedded to any visible church, could nonetheless find a religious ground of being, a transcendent locus, a mythic unity. Of the many ways in which a people might address that question, chapter 4 portrays the search that centered on two founders as heroes in life and beyond life, as biblical patriarchs or archetypes who could do for their people what Moses and Solomon did for theirs. In newness as in maturity, the United States found much that pulled apart, that separated and isolated and alienated.

Where, earnest souls asked in the eighteenth century—as in the twentieth—was unity to be found and oneness, or at least wholeness, to be secured?

REASON AND RELIGIOUS REFORMATION.

The Enlightenment introduced into America no less than into Europe a host of new religious options. In France what one thought of the Roman Catholic church was probably the best clue to which side one took in that grand contest between antiquity and modernity. In America what one thought of the Bible and the whole notion of revelation was probably the best clue to one's stance with respect to a new reformation in religion, in science, in government. Some argued (Jefferson among them) that Americans had within their grasp the opportunity for a purification of Christianity as significant as that achieved more than two centuries earlier by Luther and others.

From this perspective, religion must be tied directly to reason, with all mystery and irrational dogmatism to be dismissed forever. Moreover, religion was so closely related to morality as to be virtually identical with it. At the least, a religion that did not make signal contributions to morality was a religion unworthy of attention or acclaim. Chapter 5 speaks to the kind of religious future upon whose threshold the nation stood: a religion worthy of a free people, a religion emancipated from the knavery and deceptions of the past, a religion that transformed itself from enemy to ally of new and wondrous achievements of the human mind. Advocates of such a religion believed that they did not weaken the foundations of Western civilization or of the Christian religion, but that they substituted modern buttresses for rotting timbers.

REVELATION AND RELIGIOUS PRESERVATION.

On the other hand, many more Americans in this half century took their stand in defense of revelation and the Bible, in defense of that faith once delivered to the saints of old. Christianity stood in need not of another reformation but of a fuller and more earnest affirmation. Unlike the French Revolution, the American Revolution had not turned against the churches or their clergy, had not rejected the religious past that had guided the colonial settlements and sustained the brave settlers. Indeed, the French Revolution had demonstrated the dangers of extremism, the tragedy of unchecked violence, and the follies that follow when one turns reason into a god. This was not the path that Americans should take.

The problem with those who make so much of reason, defenders of this sixth perspective argued, is that they appoint "man the measure of all things," pushing God aside as inconsequential, if not intrusive. Theology is replaced by anthropology, since the human being is now the center of all things. In such a world, one worries no longer about salvation and God's glory, but only about human liberty and intellectual respectability. All lies within the power of the people, as the sovereignty of God is given up as a notion outmoded, belonging to the times of kings and tyrants, inquisitions and crusades. Such an attitude, it was argued, is the ancient classical sin of hubris, the old biblical sin of pride. It is as old as the Garden of Eden, where the serpent tempted the original pair to eat the fruit and become gods. In the time of our new nationhood, it is critical that we acknowledge that it is God who has made us, not we ourselves. In the matchless, wondrous universe, one must never confuse the role of the potter with the frailties of the clay.

VITALITY AND COMMUNITY.

Partaking of some elements in all the above, America's religious forces in the early decades of the nineteenth century burst forth with impressive vigor. They intended to save the West from barbarism, ignorance, and irreligion; they would inspire a nation with confidence, purpose, and godliness; they would recruit members, support ministers, build schools and colleges, dispatch missionaries, print Bibles, elevate morals, and lead all manner of reforms. Some would even take advantage of new lands and new laws to create utopian communities that could become models for the larger society to emulate. As chapter 6 indicates, both energy and idealism abounded in these early years of new nationhood.

The forces went forward in such power guided by three convictions: first, of course, that they were partners in God's plan for the age and the nation; second, that removing governmental support and sanction would prove to be a great benefit, not a heavy liability; and third, that even with a multiplicity of religious options a kind of unity in action or community of commitment could be achieved. In these years, one sensed no failure of nerve but, on the contrary, an effusion of confidence. Plurality would only stimulate vitality, and community would somehow emerge out of the factions of denominationalism, the chasms of race and gender, and the divisions of economic standing and political persuasion and intellectual sophistication. Private virtue would lead to public virtue, thus assisting the republic to survive. Private good would always be weighed in the light of public good, for a republic not committed to the commonweal could not long endure.

One finds not simplicity but complexity in this half century, just as one finds choices that are truly momentous in their consequences. One also finds enormous confidence: confidence in the value of a social order, in the power of personal piety, in the fundamental rectitude of religious liberty, in the limitless potential of the nation, in the reforming potency of reason, in the enduring place of divine transcendence, and in the prophetic voice of vital religion. It is that confidence which most separates the early years of the nineteenth century from the latter years of the twentieth. We blame our uncertainty and failure of nerve on the multiplicity and magnitude of the options confronting us. But in that respect, the generation of '76 can surely claim first place. Was the confidence of that generation and the one succeeding it born of naïveté, newness, delusions of grandeur, unreflecting zeal? Believing that faith can move mountains, leaders and followers proceeded to move them, giving us thereby our surrounding familiar landscape. We move about thereon timidly, tentatively, uncertainly, sometimes even viewing the terrain with hostility or suspicion. How did we get where we are, and where do we go from here?

Hard questions, by their nature, do not have easy answers, but ignoring those who shaped our world is to court wrong answers or to settle for no answers at all. Between 1776 and 1826 many course-plotting, compass-setting decisions were made, in religion as in politics. Understanding those decisions, as well as the choices not made and the roads not taken, can enlarge our sympathies and contribute to our wisdom. Such understanding might even restore our confidence, nerving us for the realization that we too have it in our power to reshape or redeem the land.

2. The Colonies and Their Churches

After the American Revolution, so much was new that one can miss the newness unless reminded of all that was old, familiar, accepted, axiomatic. In the final years of the twentieth century, it is easy to persuade ourselves that a comprehension of American history requires going back no farther than, say, the Age of Jackson—surely no earlier than the inauguration of George Washington. But when that latter event took place in 1789, the British colonies of North America had nearly two centuries of history behind them. Or, to put it another way, the period from Jamestown to Washington's assumption of office would stretch in the other direction from Washington's presidency to that of Richard Nixon. Such is the apologia, if one be needed, for taking the nation's colonial antecedents seriously. In the arena of religion, particularly, it is otherwise impossible to understand the one revolution in American history that was truly radical.

In all European settlements in North and in South America, the interests of state and church melded together in a strong and seemingly indissoluble bond. Today's historians put questions to yesterday's conditions that would make little sense to those who lived in sixteenth-century Mexico City, or seventeenth-century Boston, or eighteenth-century Quebec. We of today ask where the state left off and the church began; they of yesterday can only shake their heads in wonderment at so meaningless a question. It is like asking where culture starts or society stops. The truths that were self-evident to Thomas Jefferson were far from self-evident to the churchmen and the statesmen of an earlier age. On the contrary, what was self-evident to the vast majority of the colonists and their leaders (religious or political) was that society survived only as church and state worked and worshiped together, only as values were shared, only as common assumptions about human nature and the nature of God and the universe underlay all action—or at least all rationalization.

The Church of England would simply and surely go wherever the nation of England went. Such a pattern was self-evidently the case, whether we speak of France or Spain, Holland or Sweden, England before Cromwell or England after. No one defended the practice, because no one had to: it was a given of European and of Europe-in-American life. It was also a given that "savages," so long denied the blessing of the Christian gospel, should have that blessing bestowed upon them. And to reject that great gift made as little sense as for starving multitudes to turn away from freely offered food. To attack the Church as it went about its proper mission, whether to savages or civilized, was to attack the state and to threaten the very survival of civilization itself. Error had no rights, any more than deadly viruses have rights. One was either part of society—politically, morally, theologically—or one was the enemy of that society.

This is the very different world that we must first comprehend before turning attention to those leaders who so strikingly re-shaped it. In the British colonies of North America, this self-evident worldview manifested itself in two powerful versions: the Congregational Way found in New England, and the Anglican Way found, to some degree, nearly everywhere else. Risking a scandalous superficiality, one might even argue that these were merely two versions of the same Christian establishment, the chief difference being that one looked to London for direction and sup-port and the other did not. It is far more complicated than that, of course, but for our present purposes it is useful to see these two establishments as sharing a common and virtually unquestioned view of the way in which God ordered the world. The Lutherans who came to America also so believed, as did the Presbyterians, the Dutch and German Reformed, and the Roman Catholics; these groups, however, never had the opportunity in colonial America to transform their establishmentarian assumptions into political

realities of any consequence. So Anglicanism and Congregationalism more or less divided the territory between them, the former
making concessions to the Dutch in New York and New Jersey,
the latter presenting at times a united front with the Presbyterians.
In between or all around these state churches were pockets of
dissent and distraction: believers who either fled from society
altogether or were determined to organize it upon disturbingly
different assumptions. We shall return to the dissenters later.

The majority, these dominant consensus religionists, knew beyond cavil that society prospered and the gospel advanced only as
sacred and secular realms coalesced. In Virginia, the Church of
England had its earliest start, and there it achieved its most obvious colonial presence. With legislative backing by 1619, with the
passive support of the bishop of London and the more active
support of missionaries from England a century later, Anglicanism
was by 1750 stronger in the Chesapeake region than anywhere
else in the British colonies of North America. Maryland and Virginia had at that time more than half of the Anglican parishes
(about 150) that were to be found in all America. The Middle
Colonies could boast of sixty such parishes in 1750, and even New
England by this time had been successfully invaded—though not
without protest—by more than forty churches. In both of these
latter regions, expansion of the Church of England stemmed directly from the efforts of the Society for the Propagation of the
Gospel and, to a lesser extent, the Society for Promoting Christian
Knowledge.

The significance or impact of an Anglican establishment extending from Georgia to New York varied enormously from colony to
colony as well as from decade to decade. The South enjoyed the
strongest Anglican presence, but even in Virginia the complaints
of both clergy and laity painted a gloomy picture. Of course, no
bishop was present to enforce discipline, to facilitate ordination,
to defend clerical prerogatives and power. The long tenure of
Commissary James Blair in Virginia (from 1689 to his death in
1743) should have filled the episcopal vacuum more effectively
than it did; unfortunately, however, Blair and a succession of royal

governors more often worked against each other than in harmony. More crippling even than the hierarchical weakness was the parish structure. Scattered and dispersed population prevented the creation of the typical English parish, as minister after minister complained about the long distances they had to travel and the meager congregations that gathered to hear them.

Virginia's legislature, moreover, seemed unsympathetic to the uncertainty of clerical salaries, which fluctuated as the price of tobacco rose or fell. Although the law saw to it that parishes were laid out, the law could not guarantee either the success of the parish or the comfort of the minister. Success or failure at that level normally fell into the hands of the vestry, who often assumed control of the parish with such authority that many clergymen believed themselves to be more manipulated than benefited by such an arrangement. The vestry, on the other hand, had its complaints too: about clergy that left England to escape debts or wives or onerous duties, seeing Virginia as a place of retirement or refuge. It is certainly true that seventeenth-century Virginia had limited appeal for England's wealthy or well-to-do. A 1633 English pamphlet even asserted that criminals given the choice of hanging or being sent to Virginia often chose the former.[1] One can therefore speak of Anglican "rule" in Virginia only in two limited senses: Anglicans before 1750 had a virtual monopoly on the institutional religious life of Virginia; and Anglicans were more "at home," more pervasive, and more deeply rooted in Virginia than anywhere else.

The other southern colony where the Church of England was quite strong by 1750, Maryland, started out under altogether different religious auspices: namely, those of English Catholics. Lord Baltimore's proprietorship was repeatedly challenged and was ultimately lost when Maryland became a royal colony in the final decade of the seventeenth century. At that point, the three Anglican clergy already in the colony petitioned the bishop of London (in 1696) to strike while the iron was hot, strengthening the "Ecclesiastical rule here" with enough power and authority to thwart Lord Baltimore's authority permanently. If this not be done, the

clergymen warned, then Maryland will be overrun by "enthusiasts" (meaning Quakers), "idolaters" (meaning Roman Catholics), and "atheists" (meaning all nonchurchgoers in general).[2]
Thomas Bray, founder of the two missionary societies already
mentioned as important for the expansion of Anglican influence
in Maryland and Virginia, did in fact come to Maryland, though
his greatest influence was back in London as successful promoter
of the Anglican cause in all of Britain's colonies. Maryland continued to be a Catholic center in North America, but by mid-
eighteenth century three times as many Anglican churches as
Catholic ones could be found there.

Elsewhere in the South, Anglicanism had a firm foothold in
South Carolina, especially in and around the Charleston area.
North Carolina was regarded as wild and inhospitable country,
suitable for settlement only by Quakers and New Light Baptists.
Even by mid-eighteenth century Anglicans were still outnumbered there, so much so that English churchmen saw North Carolina as the best possible example of what happens to a society that
enjoys no national or established church: drunkenness, immoral-
ity, ignorance, false teaching, and scandalous worship all prevail.
True religion was insulted, along with all reason and common
sense, by that which pretended to be religion but which was, in
fact, the grossest "Exhibition of Folly that has yet appear'd in the
World."[3] Georgia, the only one of the colonies to be founded in
the eighteenth century, had by 1750 only three Anglican parishes,
and all Anglicans could only agree with the 1768 comment of one
of their own: namely, that Georgia settlers had "but very little
more knowledge of a Savior than the aboriginal natives."[4] In all
southern colonies except Maryland, the Church of England had
been favored from the beginning; yet, in all southern colonies
except Virginia, a truly established church was more hope than
reality. And even in Virginia, one could claim effectiveness only
in comparative terms.

In the Middle Colonies, Anglicanism, which had not been in on
the ground floor, quickly made up for lost time. The Dutch had,

of course, initiated settlements and trade in the New York–New Jersey regions. After only about forty years of Dutch control, however, the English seized power in 1664. Since the Dutch Reformed church was, like Anglicanism, a national establishment, the conquerers extended a courteous toleration to the conquered. Dutch Reformed parishioners continued, therefore, to be a significant presence in the eastern portions of these two states, their churches still outnumbering the Anglican ones in 1750 by more than two to one. Quite apart from the Dutch, however, Anglican authorities were unable to resist the encroachment of Congregationalists, Presbyterians, and Baptists; Anglicanism prospered in New York and New Jersey, but never did it enjoy a religious monopoly or even a comfortable majority.

Pennsylvania, launched under Quaker supervision, proved receptive to Anglicanism, as to all religions, under a deliberate policy of liberty; and tiny Delaware (or the "lower counties") had by 1750 more Anglican churches than North Carolina and Georgia combined. But here too Anglicanism never knew the security of unchallenged dominance. Dissent, diversity, heterogeneity—these nipped at the heels of a national church unaccustomed to so disorderly a bounty of religions.

To correct what was clearly an irregular state of affairs, Anglicans in the Middle Colonies more than anywhere else argued passionately, then desperately, for a bishop to reside in their midst. A bishop would set things right; a bishop would bring order out of chaos; a bishop would put enthusiasts, idolaters, and atheists in their place. Ironically, by pressing the episcopacy issue with such fervor, Anglicans nullified much of their gains hard won earlier in the eighteenth century. As the passions of the patriots increased in the 1760s and early 1770s, the obsession of Middle Colony Anglicans for strong bishops called attention to their Tory stance as well as to their assumption that episcopacy and monarchy went hand in hand. A New York Anglican, Thomas Bradbury Chandler, in his 1767 *Appeal to the Public,* alarmed more than he persuaded when he noted that

Episcopacy and Monarchy are, in their Frame and Constitution best suited to each other. Episcopacy can never thrive in a Republican Government, nor Republican Principles in an Episcopal Church. For the same Reasons, in a mixed Monarchy, no Form of Ecclesiastical Government can so exactly harmonize with the State, as that of a qualified Episcopacy.[5]

It would be difficult to imagine a less propitious time, two years after a Stamp Act had been passed and a Stamp Act Congress called, to remind the citizens of New York (and elsewhere) that the Church of England was inextricably wed to the king of England.

Growing revolutionary sentiment aggravated the problems of Anglican establishment in the Middle Colonies far more than in the South. The roots of Middle Colony Anglicanism were shallow, most of the clergy being employed as temporary missionaries by the Society for the Propagation of the Gospel. As the patriotism of this church came increasingly into question, outspoken Anglicans only darkened their church's prospects by voicing their disapproval of patriotic sentiment. When the Revolution did break out, Charles Inglis of New York's Trinity Church called it "certainly one of the most causeless, unprovoked, and unnatural [rebellions] that ever disgraced any country."[6] No wonder, then, as one Anglican missionary reported in 1776, that these unsympathetic clergy were, on occasion, "dragged from their horses, assaulted with stones & dirt, ducked in water; obliged to flee for their lives, driven from habitations & families, laid under arrest and imprisoned!"[7] In an effort to make establishment more real, these Anglican clergy had succeeded only in making it more terrifying.

In New England, Anglicanism never really had a chance to win wide public favor. Puritans and Pilgrims came to the New World for the express purpose of getting as far away as possible from a corrupt (as they saw it) Church of England, this fact setting a certain tone. Then when the Church of England did arrive in Boston, it arrived at the point of a sword. Sir Edmund Andros, surely one of the most unpopular royal governors ever to rule in North America, had the manifestly unpopular assignment of reducing the independent New Englanders into a single confederation. To all this, he added the insult of forcing upon Boston a church suitable for his own worship: King's Chapel, which opened in 1689. This thrust of Anglicanism into New England, more political than religious, did not represent the start of any surge. But the sending of missionaries early in the eighteenth century did. Rhode Island, which like Pennsylvania welcomed all religions, became the first significant center, with the Anglican missionary, James Honeyman, settling in Newport in 1704 for a stay of nearly fifty years.

Less than two decades after Honeyman's arrival, Anglicanism erupted in the very citadel of Congregationalism: Yale College. There in 1722 the rector and two tutors suddenly, scandalously, abandoned their Congregational heritage to become Anglicans and then to seek ordination back in England. Anglican missionaries could hardly take credit for this stroke of good fortune, but neither could they conceal their glee over what Honeyman called a "grand revolution." Although no wholesale defection followed, Anglicanism now grew in Connecticut as it had in Rhode Island. By the middle of the eighteenth century, Anglicanism could claim nineteen churches in Connecticut, seventeen in Massachusetts, and seven in tiny Rhode Island.

By then the agents of the Society for the Propagation of the Gospel were widely scattered throughout New England, much to the dismay of Congregationalists in general and to the disgust of the Boston pastor Jonathan Mayhew in particular. Mayhew had no objection to the general purposes of the Society; indeed, he applauded them insofar as they resulted in religion reaching areas totally bereft of Christianity. But by the 1760s, Mayhew noted, the Society seemed far more interested in competing against other Christians than in preaching to the unconverted. The Society, for example, had many more missionaries in New England in 1761 (about thirty) than in all of the southern colonies "where they were so much needed." And strangely, the Society had no missionaries at all in the West Indies, "where there are so many Negro slaves in total ignorance of Christianity." Moreover, in New England the Society did not send its agents into the hinterlands or poorer towns; on the contrary, missionaries "have generally been station'd in the oldest, most populous and richest towns, where the best provision was before made for ministers; where the public worship of God was constantly and regularly upheld, and his word and sacraments duly administered according to the congregational and presbyterian modes." Anglicanism, Mayhew concluded, was not interested in spreading the gospel, but only in "setting up altar against altar."[8] Mayhew's data appeared to support his charge, as once more the issue was one of national establishment and episcopal control—not one of Christianity, on the one hand, versus paganism, on the other.

In the mainland colonies, however, genuine episcopal control always remained more the ideal than the reality. Where the Church of England was strongest, namely, Maryland and Virginia, so was local lay control. Elsewhere in the South and the Middle Colonies, the Church of England labored under the unacceptable and unfamiliar burden of being a minority church. In New England itself, notwithstanding Mayhew's anxieties and protestations, Congregationalists outnumbered Anglicans in 1750 by a proportion of about ten to one. For in New England, something akin to real establishment did prevail—but it was Puritan, not Anglican.

In Massachusetts and Connecticut, the number of Congregational churches had grown to around four hundred by 1750—a degree of saturation unmatched by any other denomination at any time in any colony. Although the term *theocracy* cannot properly be applied to these two colonies, the term *establishment* surely can. The alliance between civil and ecclesiastical forces was intimate, meaningful, and enduring. Society, politics, education were all imbued with the unmistakable imprint of the "New England mind." In the seventeenth century, homogeneity was maintained with a success unmatched elsewhere in North America. In the eighteenth century, dissent made some inroads, but toleration (chiefly of Quakers, Baptists, and Anglicans) came slowly, reluctantly, and quite unevenly. The American Revolution that had such disastrous consequences for Anglican establishment left the Congregational connection in these two colonies relatively untouched until well into the nineteenth century. Official religion in Massachusetts and Connecticut, therefore (and in less populated New Hampshire as well), did constitute colonial America's most effective alliance between church and state. In this respect, it may be contrasted with Anglicanism, whose effectiveness was limited by geography, by diversity, by a crippled polity, and by an often passive but sometimes passionate opposition.

But if Congregationalism emerges the winner in this comparison, it must be tagged the loser from the perspective of its regional limitation. Anglicanism tried, especially with the help of Thomas Bray's private societies, to be a religious presence in all thirteen colonies, and by 1750, it had in fact penetrated all thirteen. Congregationalism, on the other hand, was a powerful presence only in New England, a pitiful presence in New York and New Jersey (seven churches in 1750), a modest entry in South Carolina (four churches), and a total void everywhere else. True, some of this parochialism is mitigated by the close association between the Congregationalists and the Presbyterians. The latter were strong in the middle and southern colonies, but between the two denominations no institutional bond existed nor, at this time, any grand strategy of conquest.

Congregationalism, therefore, though it offered a model of what establishment in America might become, lacked the capacity to bestow upon that model a universal appeal. And where the model had proved effective, it had done so at the cost of intolerance and persecution that left deep scars in the social memory. If the strident calls for an English bishop created a powerful backlash against Anglicanism, Congregationalism proved for many no more attractive an alternative, since it had so often resorted to fines, whips, jails, and gallows.

The two most powerful religious bodies in the American colonies, Anglicanism and Congregationalism, had by far the greatest number of churches by mid-eighteenth century. Indeed, if the Presbyterian churches be counted with the Congregational and Anglican ones, the total by 1750 approached a thousand. All other denominations together had less than half that number.[9] From the perspective of numbers alone, one could reasonably have concluded that some pattern of church establishment would prevail, that minority and dissenting voices would be drowned out, that the only real choice after the Revolution would not be between the establishment of religion or no, but only which establishment should prevail. We know that this is not how the story turned out, and we shall soon be considering those laymen who had so much to do with that fact. But dissenters also shaped how the story came out, and not in their mere passive presence as contributors to diversity and therefore to the complexity of the choice. Their contribution was far more active, far more deliberate, far more self-conscious than that. We turn, therefore, to that small minority who resisted the "self-evidence" of establishment, those who, not on political or pragmatic grounds, but on historical and theological grounds, argued for a "full liberty in religious concernments."

Resistance to religious conformity came early. The New World represented for many who emigrated a time and a place where "the Lord hath more truth and light yet to break forth"—as Leyden's Pilgrim pastor, John Robinson, explained in 1620. That New World implied, even invited, experimentation, novelty, a readiness to heed the Spirit and follow wherever it led. This was characteristic of the Puritan vision itself, of course, which is one reason the early Puritans felt that they must deal severely with those who surrendered too readily to their own private whims, their idiosyncratic fancies. But neither alternative ways of life nor variant theologies could be restrained, especially in a wilderness. Not the broad tolerance of the rationalist, but the narrow conviction of the zealot, would first test freedom's limits in the New World. In the Old World as well, John Milton would argue in his *Areopagitica*

(1644) that truth was not set and fixed, but still unfolding; truth, even biblical truth, was a "streaming fountain" and if oppressive authorities tried to cramp one's search, then scriptural truths would "sick'n in a muddy pool of conformity and tradition."[10] There must be "perpetuall progression," "further light," endless unfolding, as Milton found the line from freedom in religion to freedom of the press to be straight and clear.

Along with Milton's English voice, some American voices cried out against any cramping of mind or soul or spirit. Ejected from Massachusetts in 1636, Roger Williams had occasion to reflect at length on the relationship between civil and churchly powers, on the demands for conformity, and on the horrors of religious persecution in human history. In Williams's view the history of England alone should have been enough to show the folly of enforced conformity, for "It hath been England's sinful shame to fashion and change her garments and religions with wondrous ease and lightness, as a higher power, a stronger sword, hath prevailed; after the ancient pattern of Nebuchadnezzar's bowing the whole world in one most solemn uniformity of worship to his golden image."[11] But Massachusetts had not learned its lesson; this New World government would, if possible, still bind the conscience, would still allow the wilderness of the world to invade the garden of Christ's church—between which, said Williams, a "wall of separation" should stand. The Bay Colony persisted in persecuting—not knowing or caring whether they just might be persecuting Christ. "I must profess," Williams exclaimed, "while heaven and earth last, that no one tenent that either London, England, or the world doth harbor is so heretical, blasphemous, seditious, and dangerous to the corporal, to the spiritual, to the present, to the eternal good of all men as the bloody tenent . . . of persecution for cause of conscience."[12]

Such passion did not result from a mere private quarrel between Roger Williams and John Cotton over the way that Massachusetts ought to run its own affairs and to handle the "affair" of Williams. Here was a principle, not an apologia; a conviction concerning a God-given right, not a calculated defense. When an uneducated and powerless Baptist named Obadiah Holmes left Rhode Island in 1651 on a private preaching mission to Massachusetts, that lowly man was arrested, tried, convicted, and publicly whipped in Boston with thirty lashes. Holmes had not the eloquence to defend himself; Williams supplied the eloquence, together with white-hot indignation, in a letter to the colony's governor as he condemned this outrageous violation of conscience. "The Maker and Searcher of our hearts knows," Williams wrote, "with what bitterness I write." Now, fifteen years after his own involuntary exile, Williams learned that the Bay Colony was corrupt still. It would stubbornly persist in following the bloody and unsavory path that England had for a hundred years or more pursued. And to what end? Pure religion? True Christianity? Nonsense! "Sir, I must be humbly bold to say that 'tis impossible for any man or men to maintain their Christ by their sword and to worship a true Christ . . . and not to fight against God . . . and to hunt after the precious life of the true Lord Jesus Christ." Williams concluded by calling for a spirit of moderation together with a resolve, "in these wonderful searching, disputing, and dissenting times," for those in authority to search, listen, pray, fast, and "tremblingly to enquire what the holy pleasure and the holy mysteries of the most Holy are." In other words, sir, please resolve to be less certain that you are beyond all question absolutely and unfailingly right.[13]

Obadiah Holmes returned to Newport, whipped but not whipped down, to join once more with John Clarke in leading a Baptist church that would keep consciences free. John Clarke accompanied Roger Williams to England in order to secure for Rhode Island a charter that guaranteed "a full liberty in religious concernments" to all its citizens. This charter, secured in 1663, offered the most explicit guarantee of religious liberty that the New World had yet seen: no one should be molested, punished, or disquieted for "any difference of opinion in matters of religion," but on the contrary, all persons shall "freely and fully have and enjoy . . . their own judgments and consciences."[14]

Rhode Island would differ as sharply as possible from neighboring Connecticut and Massachusetts, not simply in being more tolerant, not merely in adjusting to diversity, but far more than that in proclaiming a religious liberty as complete and unflinching as has been achieved anywhere in the world more than three centuries later. Government did not exist to destroy liberty of conscience, but to preserve and protect it.

So Rhode Island would protect even the Quakers who came to live there and would soon dominate the government. Roger Williams did not like the Quakers; he despised their theology and distrusted their motives. In all this, he was not alone. He was alone, however, in asserting that their consciences should nonetheless be left free. In Quakerism's early decades of the 1650s and 1660s, the Spirit-filled enthusiasts were deemed to be as much a political and social threat as a theological one. Massachusetts could not abide in its midst those fanatics who pretended to a private revelation from God, those zealots who paid no heed to biblical reproof or clerical censure. No government could long endure in the face of anarchists who accepted no authority except that within their own breasts. So Massachusetts cropped their ears and burned their tongues; then the Bay Colony exiled them; then, it hanged them.

In the eyes of establishment, any religious establishment, once again error had no rights. And once again, the pattern had been set in the Old World over and over, in countless inquisitions, tortures, condemnations, and burnings at the stake. During its civil war, England had seen more diversity in religion than it had ever cared to dream of. With the restoration of the monarchy in 1660, the nation again moved to contain, suppress, or eradicate the more extreme forms of nonconformity to the Church of England. Quakerism was precisely such an unholy zeal. As all the axioms of Western civilization made perfectly evident, Quakers therefore had to be suppressed.

Quakers, along with other revolutionaries of the Cromwellian era, terrified the forces of law and order. With the Restoration in 1660 came the resolve to set English society once more on a safe and sober course. The Clarendon Code was designed to do precisely that, as it provided fines, jails, social ostracism, and other forms of discouragement to dissent. Perhaps the most famous prisoner of the Code's several measures, John Bunyan, achieved his first notoriety by attacking the Quakers. Even that could not endear him to the crown, however, for he too dissented from the Church of England, its theology, its polity, its liturgy. Bunyan could attack the Quakers in print; he had no other weapon. The government, however, could move with force against these naked revolutionaries whose principal crime was to call England back to righteousness. By restoring the king and his bishops, most of the English believed they had already returned to righteousness. In any case, they resolved to end all enthusiastic bombast as swiftly and definitively as possible. Quakers must be brought to heel— suppressed, or if possible obliterated. Were it not for the prestige and conviction of a William Penn, together with the inviting wilderness of a New World, this might indeed have happened.

Quakers in the 1660s and 1670s proved to be an easy and vulnerable target for persecution in England and Ireland. Their presence was obvious and their preaching obnoxious; no more than that was needed to make the case against them. Penn, who had difficulty with such reasoning, presented in 1670 a striking attack against it: *The Great Case of Liberty of Conscience.* Here he freely acknowledged his status as a religious dissenter but asked how this offended the civil government or dishonored the nation. Though his argument implicitly defended all dissenters, the "poor despised Quakers" would he specifically rescue.

For mine own part, I publickly confess myself to be a very hearty Dissenter from the established worship of these nations . . . [I believe Quakers] to be the undoubted followers of Jesus Christ, in his most holy, strait, and narrow way, that leads to the eternal rest. In all which I know no treason, nor any principle that would urge me to a thought injurious to the civil peace. If any be defective in this particular, it is equal [just] both individuals and whole societies should answer for their own defaults; but we are clear.[15]

Arguing from every basis that he could expect rational and Christian rulers to acknowledge, Penn patiently explained that each violation of liberty of conscience managed only "to impeach the honor of God, the meekness of the Christian religion, the authority of scripture, the privilege of nature, the principles of common reason, the well being of government," and aggravate the "apprehensions of the greatest personages" of the past and the future.[16]

Less than a dozen years later, Penn seized the opportunity to do more than write in defense of the Quakers. He became the instrument for providing them with a vast refuge where liberty of conscience was built into the very frame of government. When Penn in 1682 published his first set of laws for the newly founded Pennsylvania, section 35 read as follows:

That all persons living in this province who confess and acknowledge the one almighty and eternal God to be the creator, upholder, and ruler of the world, and that hold themselves obliged in conscience to live peaceably and justly in civil society, shall in no ways be molested or prejudiced for their religious persuasion or practice in matters of faith and worship, nor shall they be compelled at any time to frequent or maintain any religious worship, place, or ministry whatever.[17]

The Jeffersonian parallels in the latter portion of this legislation may be noted, whereas the earlier phrases affirm a kind of belief that even the deist could accept. Penn clearly revealed more concern than any deist did, however, for religious practice and religious worship. At the same time, the freedom not to worship was explicit, though these early laws did provide that all persons abstain "from their common daily labor" on "the Lord's Day."[18]

Penn, of course, was neither a Madisonian nor a Jeffersonian deist. The point, rather, is that however much honor is given to these and other founding fathers, we must not forget believers such as Penn and Williams who would defend liberty of conscience because religion was too precious a commodity to be bought and sold, or traded to the highest bidder, or surrendered to the strongest sword. And Penn's colony, it soon became clear, would be a refuge not for Quakers alone but for all those of tender conscience. Before a century of such unusual freedom had passed, Pennsylvania found within its borders an unbelievable hodgepodge of religious groups: there were Catholics, Protestants, Jews, but that hardly began to exhaust a list that included Anglicans, Baptists, Presbyterians, Methodists, Lutherans, Moravians, Mennonites, Brethren, Schwenkfelders, and more.

Even more unbelievable than the fact that such a melange could live side by side without killing each other was the staggering evidence that Pennsylvania actually prospered. Though it started much later than such colonies as Connecticut and Virginia, which labored to preserve their establishments, Pennsylvania grew stronger and richer—so it seemed—by the hour. William Penn spoke eloquently on the subject of liberty of conscience, but the prosperity of his colony spoke even more eloquently and persuasively. Was it just possible that society and economy could flourish without an establishment of religion? Of course it was possible, even plausible: behold Pennsylvania! It is improper to suggest that Penn's colony had no problems, that diversity led to perfect harmony, that Quaker pacifism was not both resisted and resented, that Anglican missionaries could readily adjust to so wild a swarm of fanatics, that denominations themselves did not further quarrel and divide. But, despite all, *Pennsylvania prospered.* Rhode Island could demonstrate what liberty of conscience meant for the individual; Pennsylvania demonstrated what it meant for society.

Just south of Pennsylvania, and precisely how far south was a matter of great contention, the flame of religious liberty flickered for a time in Lord Baltimore's Maryland. One half century before the grant of Charles II to William Penn, Charles I had bestowed a much smaller parcel of land upon the Calvert family. Lord Baltimore hardly needed to be reminded of the chief problem that confronted him: namely, that he was a Roman Catholic dwelling in a vigilantly Protestant realm. Nor did he need to be reminded that it required courage in the extreme for him to bring an English Catholic colony into being where Protestant Virginia lay immediately to his south, Puritan New England somewhat more remotely to his north. Maryland might well be suspected of encouraging Roman Catholic Spain "or some other forraigne enemy to suppresse the Protestants in those parts, or perhaps grow strong enough to doe it of themselves."[19] From politics if not from principle, Lord Baltimore recognized that Maryland could not be a Catholic "refuge" in the way that Pennsylvania proved later to be a Quaker one. Land could not be sold only to English Catholics, nor could the voices in government be exclusively Catholic. From the beginning, Catholic and Protestant must learn to live together peaceably, to be good neighbors, good citizens, good laborers. Even on the first ships sailing to the Chesapeake, Baltimore indicated what his *modus vivendi* would be, instructing that all acts of Roman Catholic religion aboard ship "be done as privately as may be," that all Roman Catholics "be silent upon all occasions of discourse concerning matters of religion."[20] A religious minority, especially a politically suspect religious minority, must not give offense to a powerful nation allied with a powerful church.

Baltimore's problems were wider than that, to be sure, and every act of charity seemed to be answered by intrigue or rebellion against him. As early as the 1640s, William Claiborne wrested control from Baltimore's hands, expelling any Jesuit unlucky enough to be identified. Back in control by 1646, Baltimore invited more Protestants to settle in Maryland, thinking thereby to allay suspicion and encourage a prosperous growth. In 1649, he supported the passage of an Act of Toleration designed to settle the ever-threatening religious war between Protestant and Catholic. That act provided that "no persons professing to believe in Jesus Christ should be molested in respect of their religion, or in the free exercise thereof, or be compelled to the belief or exercise of any other religion, against their consent."[21] Except for its christological tone, this act echoed language that would become far more familiar in the second half of the eighteenth century. Its line of direct influence, however, was broken by persisting and enlarging difficulties in Baltimore's effective proprietorship: England's civil war, Pennsylvania's encroachment, and the Glorious Revolution, which exchanged the deeply resented Catholicism of James II for the more politic Protestantism of William III. After Maryland was declared a royal colony in 1691, Anglican forces lost little time in making this once-Catholic colony their very own. Parishes were laid out, vestries appointed, commissaries (Thomas Bray) invited, and soon missionaries sent forth. Though Roman Catholicism remained an underground force in Maryland for the rest of the colonial period, the colony no longer had the chance to bear effective witness to those liberties peculiar to conscience.

By the time that Anglicanism asserted itself in Maryland, England had asserted its own measure of religious toleration. The Act of Toleration of 1689 preserved the privileges and unique status of the Church of England, but it brought an end to the long and unhappy history of the bloodiest forms of religious persecution. Its effect in the colonies was quite uneven, however, with some authorities arguing that the provisions did not even apply, others only seeing to it that they were not applied. In fact, the development of religious liberty in America, or even of religious toleration, moved most unsteadily through the first half of the eighteenth century. Congregationalism maintained its position in New England, while Anglicanism strengthened its hold not only in Maryland but in all of the Middle Colonies as well.

By the middle of the eighteenth century, the forces of establishment appeared even stronger than before. Rhode Island and Pennsylvania were pockets of liberty, but the strong voices of Williams and Penn had long been stilled. Then an eruption of popular piety stirred religious passions throughout all of the colonies and within a great many of the churches. Establishment seemed threatened not by legislation or regicide, but by that Spirit which blows where it will, breaking out of all the socially approved forms. No establishment, foreign or domestic, was strong enough to say "only here, and not there." Having one's credentials approved did not mean nearly so much as having one's heart warmed. Being the pastor of a major parish was not nearly so important as being preacher to the whole waiting world. To some, this new zeal seemed like the Cromwellian madness all over again, with fanatics and enthusiasts ready to turn society and the whole political order upside down.

Because of efforts to stem the tide, the initial effect of this Great Awakening on religious liberty was negative. Connecticut, for example, passed laws in 1742 that virtually nullified earlier timid steps toward toleration. Congregationalists who withdrew from the Standing Order to create Separatist churches no longer benefited from earlier acts of toleration, and when such schismatic Congregationalists chose to call themselves Baptists, those earlier acts were repealed altogether. Defenders of establishment argued that they were simply trying to preserve society and promote peace. Well, yes, one Separatist responded: Congregationalists are for peace "upon the same terms that the Pope is for peace, for he wants to rule over all Christians throughout the whole world." If these high and mighty leaders prevail in Connecticut or elsewhere in New England, then "separates and Baptists would have no more liberties here than the protestants have in France or Rome."[22]

Others, moved to question more than mere motivation, reflected on the whole nature of church-state relationships. A leading Separatist, Solomon Paine, decided by 1752 that this whole notion of alliance was theologically wrong:

The cause of a just separation of the saints from their fellow men in their worship, is not that there are some hypocrites in the visible church of Christ, nor that some fall into scandalous sins in the Church, nor because the minister is flat, formal, or even saith he is a minister of Christ, and is not, and doth lie; but it is their being yoked together, or incorporated into a corrupt constitution, under the government of another supreme head than believers, which will not purge out any of the corrupt fruit, but naturally bears it and nourishes it, and denies the power of godliness, both in the government and gracious effects of it.[23]

Here is language far closer to Roger Williams than to Thomas Jefferson, but now closer in time to the latter than the former. For pietists awakened by the revival or for new churches brought into existence by this Awakening, for New Lights and New Side and all New Born, what does Christ have to do with Satan? Come out, and be separate.[24] Thus saith not John Locke, but the Lord. Also, and this is important for the whole revolutionary period, thus saith not the learned and the mighty, but the foolish and the lowly.

Though the Congregational establishment held so far as its laws were concerned, that establishment slipped so far as shifting public sentiments were concerned. Anglicanism also maintained its internal structure intact in all the turbulence of revivalism and unchecked emotion. By holding itself aloof from the movement, however, the Church of England isolated itself more and more from its potential flock. It took refuge in its liturgy, cultivated its patronage, and grew ever more insistent on having its episcopacy in full working order in America. The main effect of the Awakening on Anglicanism was to make it appear increasingly "flat, formal" (to quote Paine) and correspondingly remote from the concerns of most Americans. Anglican ministers reported to their superiors in London that in all the furies of this revivalism "the Church . . . stood steady in that Storm."[25] So it did, but the storm covered—and carried—much of the land.

Anglicanism suffered even more, of course, as revolutionary passions grew. As the rhetoric against England's Parliament and king increased in volume and scorn, some of those harsh words fell upon England's church. Missionaries of the Society for the Propagation of the Gospel were regularly Tory. When Chandler wrote in 1767 that "Episcopacy and Monarchy are, in their Frame and Constitution, best suited to each other," and that "Episcopacy can never thrive in a Republican Government, nor Republican Principles in an Episcopal Church,"[26] he alienated all potential patriots. Somehow, Chandler convinced himself that this line of argument made a logic-tight case for sending bishops to America. No bishops ever came, but a revolution did, and the effect on Anglicanism was both swift and devastating.

The Congregational establishment faced a different set of problems. Its loyalty was not in question; its good judgment and its charity were. And just as anti-England rhetoric spilled over onto that nation's church, so pro-liberty rhetoric spilled over onto a

New England Way that seemed peculiarly, stubbornly resistant to the idea of "a full liberty in religious concernments." Some dissenters underlined this inconsistency. Isaac Backus, for one, noted in 1774 that "taxation without representation" had its application in the religious no less than the political realm. To the Massachusetts legislature, he pointed out what to the dissenters seemed so obvious:

That which has made the greatest noise, is a tax of three pence a pound on tea; but your law of last June laid a tax of the same sum every year upon the Baptists in each parish. . . . And only because the Baptists in Middleboro' have refused to pay that little tax, we hear that the first parish in said town have this fall voted to lay a greater tax upon us. All Americans are alarmed at the tea tax; though, if they please, they can avoid it by not buying tea; but we have no such liberty. We must either pay the little tax, or else your people appear even in this time of extremity, determined to lay a greater one upon us. But these lines are to let you know, that we are determined not to pay either of them; not only upon your principles of not being taxed where we are not represented, but also because we dare not render that homage to any earthly power, which I and many of my brethren are fully convinced belongs only to God.[27]

When earlier in 1774 Backus had made similar points to the Continental Congress gathered in Philadelphia, John Adams thought the whole discussion trivial, since establishment in New England was such a "slender thing."[28] Establishment in New England was not really worth worrying about, the defenders of the Standing Order argued; certainly it was not to be spoken of in the same breath with Anglican establishment. That benign view, however, was not shared by the dissenters in New England, nor even by John Adams in his old age. By the time of the Revolution, dissenting voices could be heard throughout the British colonies arguing against establishment anytime, anywhere. In Virginia, for example, Presbyterians and Baptists protested against the Anglican establishment by flooding the legislature with wave after wave of petitions; beyond that, however, these dissenters forcefully and passionately argued for a full and complete liberty in matters of religious conscience. Such voices regarded this liberty as more critical than trade laws or parliamentary presumption or unjust taxes. Liberty there must be of both body and soul. Just as civil and ecclesiastical tyranny had gone hand in hand to enslave humanity, so political and religious liberty must join together to emancipate the world.

But the Revolution was really about politics, not about religion—or so the familiar argument runs. And to the extent that it dealt with ideas, the ideas were those of radical Whigs (were they not?) rather than of consistent Calvinists. Yet, radical Whigs were only dissenting Protestants, once removed. As Robert Middlekauf has pointed out, "Radical Whig perceptions of politics attracted widespread support in America because they revived the traditional concerns of a Protestant culture that had always verged on Puritanism." Those concerns included a despair over luxurious self-indulgence and arbitrary exercise of power, a hope for a social and political order in which passion was restrained and virtue was pursued. "The generations that made the Revolution were the children of the twice-born, the heirs of this seventeenth-century religious tradition."[29]

Before turning to the heroic and herculean labors of Jefferson and Madison, we should fix firmly in our minds the concurrent tradition of religious liberty stemming from the Miltons and Williamses and Penns, a tradition that challenged the self-evident truths of establishment, be they Catholic or Calvinist, Lutheran or Anglican. William Lee Miller has even argued recently that this "broad river of history—let us call it dissenting Protestantism—had more to do, over all, over time, pound for pound, head for head, with the shaping of the American tradition of religious liberty than did the rational Enlightenment."[30] Though that may be true, it is likewise true that dissenting Protestantism could not by itself have successfully stormed the gates of establishment. More power was required, more troops needed to bring down alliances of church and state, for behind those alliances stood all the force of history, all the authority of received wisdom, all the assurance of axiomatic truth. Against entrenched positions of such potency and hoary respectability, only a mighty counterthrust could hope to nudge a reluctant world away from its bloodied soil of persecution toward a higher ground where all consciences might be free.

3. The Libertarians: Jefferson and Madison

Thomas Jefferson (1743–1826) and James Madison (1751–1836) came to know each other in Williamsburg politics and lived not far from each other in Piedmont provincialism. But when their "great collaboration" was finished,[1] few would think of either man in terms so local or restrictive or limited. Deeply committed to their own time and place, Jefferson and Madison transcended both, moving far beyond the boundaries of Virginia and the decades of their own life spans.

Jefferson, a graduate of the College of William and Mary, was elected to the House of Burgesses when still in his twenties and later to the Continental Congress, where his activity in 1776 has become a legend. Minister to France in the late 1780s, he served as secretary of state and then vice-president in the 1790s, all this service to be followed by two terms as president in the first decade of the nineteenth century. Madison, a graduate of Princeton, also served in the Continental Congress, then in the Constitutional Convention, where his contribution was critical and his defense of the labors of that Convention historic. He was elected to the First Congress assembled under the new Constitution, then served two terms as secretary of state, this to be followed by two terms as president. Both men had public careers of vast scope and impact, but those bare biographical bones will have to suffice. For our concern here is not primarily with their office holding, but with their unwavering vision of and unrelenting activity regarding the proper limits of religious power in all earthly affairs.

By separate though similar routes of reasoning, Jefferson and Madison came to understand much of western European history as needlessly besmirched and tragically bloodied by the heavy hand of despotic religion. So also in Virginia, Jefferson found the Church of England much too privileged and protected, with the virtually automatic result that it became pompous, persecutorial, and far more involved in political than in spiritual concerns. Madison, at the tender age of twenty-two, already found himself out of patience with neighboring Anglicans who indulged in that "diabolical, hell-conceived principle of persecution."[2] By jailing half a dozen "well-meaning men" for merely proclaiming their religious opinions, Madison's neighbors unwittingly launched a career committed to liberty in religion. It was his very first libertarian concern; it was to be his last. "Pity me, and pray for liberty of conscience to all," Madison wrote in early 1774.[3]

A few months later to this same college chum, William Bradford, Jr., of Philadelphia, Madison compared the liberality of Pennsylvania with the intolerance of Virginia. When one considered religious liberty, he wrote, our two colonies might as well be on different continents. "The Sentiments of our people of Fortune & fashion on this subject are vastly different from what you have been used to. That liberal catholic and equitable way of thinking as to the rights of Conscience, which is one of the Characteristics of a free people and so strongly marks the People of your province is but little known among the Zealous adherents to our Hierarchy."[4] Pennsylvania, Madison pointed out, enjoyed many successes, and certainly this must be seen as "the good effects of their religious as well as Civil Liberty." We in Virginia, on the other hand, cling to our establishment, abuse our dissenters, and dampen our natural genius. "Religious bondage shackles and debilitates the mind and unfits it for every noble enterprize, every expanded prospect."[5] On this dimension of liberty, Madison required no instruction from Jefferson, who was eight years his senior. Madison's education under John Witherspoon, together with his extensive reading in religion during early periods of ill health, convinced him that reason, not power, was the only legitimate ally of religion. Arguments he would hear; imprisonments and threats he would despise.

When independence was declared in July of '76, Virginia immediately set about to exchange the old colonial and royal government for a new self-administered and republican one. Jefferson, so much concerned for what would happen in this "his country" that he could hardly tear himself away for Philadelphia, proposed a constitution for Virginia that would give liberty its firmest protection. Convinced that religious liberty must, most assuredly, be built into the structural frame of the new government, Jefferson proposed this language: "All persons shall have full and free liberty of religious opinion; nor shall any be compelled to frequent or maintain any religious institution": freedom *for* religion, but also freedom *from* religion. This language was not adopted in the constitution of the new state, the delegates preferring the language of George Mason, who had already provided Virginians with their own Declaration of Rights. By the end of the year, the legislature had taken other significant steps such as exempting dissenters from taxes that would go to the Anglican (Episcopal) church and dropping those provisions of English common law that required religious conformity in either behavior or belief. Though Jefferson naturally approved of these actions, he nonetheless worried that a full liberty was not explicitly guaranteed. In the year that he became governor of Virginia, 1779, Jefferson introduced a bill that would, he believed, put freedom in religion firmly on solid ground. Year after year the legislature managed to dally and dispute and balk with respect to Jeffersonian language and Jeffersonian intent.

Perhaps dissenters could be tolerated, but surely this need not mean that "Virginia's Mother Church"[6] need be cast adrift to shift for itself in a sea swarming with sectaries! Perhaps severing ties with England required readjustments, but surely not doing violence to more than a century and a half of Virginia tradition! Perhaps England's church in Virginia should reorganize itself on native soil, but surely it need not forsake all official alliances with a state that now needed its church more than ever before! Along with these "perhapses" was an even more serious presentation of alternatives. Perhaps we can no longer afford the luxury of a single established church, but surely we cannot afford the despair and inevitable degeneracy of no establishment at all! Therefore, and here was a most appealing "therefore," we shall propose Christianity itself as "the established Religion of this Commonwealth; and all Denominations of Christians demeaning themselves peaceably and faithfully shall enjoy equal privileges."

This quotation comes from a bill advanced by Patrick Henry and supported by such other worthies as John Marshall and Richard Henry Lee. In the Tidewater region of the state, where the Anglican tradition had its deepest roots and where leading Virginia families wielded great political power, Henry's Bill Establishing a Provision for Teachers of the Christian Religion cast a seductive spell.[7] But in the Piedmont and valleys of Virginia, where dissent was strong and the lust for liberty rampant, such a bill seemed only another ruse for returning once again to the repression and persecution already too well known. Backcountry Baptists urged the legislature not to rest in its push for religious liberty until "every grievous yoke be broken," and Hanover Presbyterians argued that such a proposal would be in direct violation of Virginia's own Declaration of Rights. Legislators, the Presbyterians added, should recognize their own limits in religious matters and not presume their "Supremacy in Spirituals."[8]

Backcountry protests would not of themselves defeat so alluring, so tempting an idea—especially in a legislature still heavily dominated by "first families," invariably Anglican. But perhaps someone of good family, of good education, of good mental prowess and strong conviction could help make the case against this plural establishment. James Madison is the name that must be credited for the defeat of an idea whose time had so very nearly come. And the Madison name remains indissolubly linked with that "Memorial and Remonstrance" that was the rhetorically powerful instrument of defeat.[9] A member of the legislature himself, Madison labored and lobbied against this notion of "general assessment" in argument so persuasive, in language so ringing that now, two hundred years later, it has only gained—not lost—in force. (For full text, see Appendix A.)

Religion, Madison argued, is never properly a matter for armies to decide or legislatures to promote. Only reason and conviction are relevant to decisions on who worships when or where or how—or if at all. Since this is true, neither generals nor politicians have the right or authority, much less the wisdom, to "judge of Religious Truth." Moreover, if today the state of Virginia can legitimately establish Christianity, then what is to prevent the state, tomorrow, from establishing "any particular sect of Christians, in exclusion of all other Sects?" And if we do that, well then, we are right back where we were before a Revolution was fought and a tyranny deposed. Beyond all this, what lessons has history taught us about the effects of every alliance between church and state? During almost fifteen hundred years of such connections, "What have been its fruits?" Madison asked. And he answered: "More or less in all places, pride and indolence in the Clergy, ignorance and servility in the laity; in both, superstition, bigotry and persecution." We shall be true to the principles of "the late Revolution," Madison concluded, not by constricting the bands of freedom but by ever widening them, by preserving Virginia and the whole nation as "an Asylum to the persecuted," and by leaving all laws pertaining to religion to the only truly qualified authority in this area: namely, "the Supreme Lawgiver of the Universe."

Madison had wisely taken care to get as many signatures as possible affixed to his memorial. Backcountry dissenters signed it; even some members of "the old hierarchy" signed it; persons weary of religious strife and stridency signed it. The sweet reasonableness of Henry's proposal did not now, upon further reflection and with skillful Madisonian prodding, seem either so sweet or so reasonable after all. As sentiment for establishment of any kind sputtered and died, sentiment grew for passing that long-delayed Jeffersonian bill. The legislature was still unwilling to swallow Jefferson's deism whole, so that some of his more extravagant language on the omnipotence of reason had to be toned down. But the essential guarantee of freedom in religion, even more for freedom of the human mind, stood unmitigated and undamaged. Madison, serving as brilliant legislative midwife for a Jefferson far away in Paris, managed to prevent more serious substitutions and amendments. At long last, the bill first introduced in 1779 passed both houses of the Virginia legislature on January 16, 1786. The Statute was an extraordinary triumph for the Madisonian-Jeffersonian partnership; it was also an extraordinary bequest to the nation and the world.

With the phrase "whereas Almighty God hath created the mind free" Jefferson opened his argument and set forth his basic premise. Religion had historically been a major means for shackling human minds, not emancipating them. But that age of human history now belonged to the past, along with all the hypocrisy and meanness that had accompanied government bribery and ecclesiastical coercion. Let us consider, Jefferson wrote, that if an all-wise and all-powerful God restrained himself from coercing either the bodies or the minds of men and women, how utterly absurd it must then be for "fallible and uninspired men" to assume "dominion over the faith of others." In this new enlightened age we must recognize "that our civil rights have no dependence upon our religious opinions, any more than our opinions in physics or geometry." Above all else we must have the confidence, the courage, to affirm "that truth is great and will prevail if left to herself, that she is the proper and sufficient antagonist to error, and has nothing to fear from the conflict . . . errors ceasing to be dangerous when it is permitted freely to contradict them." With these powerful presuppositions, eloquently proclaimed, the Jeffersonian Statute delivered its legislative bite:

Be it enacted by the General Assembly, That no man shall be compelled to frequent or support any religious worship, place, or ministry whatsoever, nor shall be enforced, restrained, molested, or burthened in his body or goods, nor shall otherwise suffer on account of his religious opinions or belief; but that all men shall be free to profess, and by argument to maintain, their opinion in matters of religion, and that the same shall in no wise diminish, enlarge, or affect their civil capacities. (For full text, see Appendix A.)

So strongly did Jefferson feel about this enforcing language that he, in contrast to another of his principles that the earth belonged to the living, declared that this legislative act pertained to an essential and natural right. Here was no mere law or civil regulation passed today to be amended next year or revoked the next. No, here was recognition of a fundamental human right to be assured forever!

Within one week of its passage, Madison reported to Jefferson the happy news: his bill had become law, and perhaps an end had been written, Madison added, to all attempts in Virginia's history to make "laws for the human mind."[10] Within a year, a jubilant Jefferson could announce that the whole Western world had applauded Virginia's bold assertion of freedom.

The Virginia act for religious freedom has been received with infinite approbation in Europe & propagated with enthusiasm. I do not mean by the governments, but by the individuals which compose them. It has been translated into French & Italian, has been sent to most of the courts of Europe, & has been the best evidence of the falsehood of those reports which stated us to be in anarchy. It is inserted in the new Encyclopedie, & is appearing in most of the publications respecting America. In fact it is comfortable to see the standard of reason at length erected, after so many ages during which the human mind has been held in vassalage by kings, priests & nobles: and it is honorable for us to have produced the first legislature who had the courage to declare that the reason of man may be trusted with the formation of his own opinions.[11]

Jefferson's pride of authorship does come through, as it does in his adding this Statute to the first English edition of his *Notes on the State of Virginia,* published the following year (1787). And of course that pride comes through even more emphatically when he asked to be remembered on his tombstone for the writing of only two documents: the Declaration of Independence and this Statute.

As both Jefferson and Madison realized, however, 1786 announced a beginning, not a concluding, in the long legal battle for full religious freedom. However promising the beginning, one could not relax until convinced that the Jeffersonian words were effectively and everywhere understood. In the *Notes* Jefferson elaborated his views on government's keeping its distance from all religious affairs and religious opinions. "The legitimate powers of government," he wrote, "extend to such acts only as are injurious to others. But it does me no injury for my neighbor to say that there are twenty gods, or no God. It neither picks my pocket nor breaks my leg." He added that state-protected, state-coerced religion succeeded only in making "one half the world fools, and the other half hypocrites."[12] These words, mildly shocking from a United States minister to France, provided powerful ammunition to Jefferson's enemies in a presidential campaign over a decade away. But Jefferson was not yet ready to weigh such political considerations. More urgent was the need for that freedom which Virginia had proclaimed to prevail far beyond the borders of a single state.

When delegates to the Constitutional Convention gathered in Philadelphia in May 1787, religion seemed to most of them a matter best left to the states. Traditions and practices varied so widely that discussions about religion could only lead to dissension and delaying disagreements. The delegates to the Constitutional Convention took therefore only two modest steps with respect to religion, both of these being designed to avert problems, not raise them. First, the delegates agreed that "no religious test" should ever be required of federal officeholders, and second, that one could "affirm" rather than "swear" in taking the oath of office—a clear concession to the tender consciences of Quakers. Other than that, however, the Constitution was totally silent on the subject of religion: no national church, of course, but no national affirmations of faith, either, not even of the most generalized sort. Jefferson, grateful for those omissions, expressed no gratitude for the delegates' failure to offer clear, unambiguous guarantees of religious freedom.

Madison, of course, played a determinative role in the drafting of the Constitution, the genius of the final document reflecting Madison's intimate familiarity with the best political theory of the day. Unlike Jefferson, Madison believed that assurances respecting religious and other liberties did pertain, most appropriately, to the states. When the delegates completed their work in the fall of 1787, Madison hastened to send Jefferson, still in Paris, a copy of their efforts. Jefferson, favorably impressed with the proposed constitution, offered his compliments to Madison. But then he observed: "I will now add what I do not like. First the omission of a bill of rights providing clearly and without the aid of sophisms for the freedom of religion."[13] He went on to name other freedoms, but to pause here is to emphasize the priority that Jefferson gave to what William Lee Miller has aptly called *The First Liberty*.[14] The United States in its fundamental frame of government, no less than Virginia in its, must without equivocation declare itself for full religious liberty. Madison discovered Jefferson's strong sentiment to be widespread, particularly among Virginia's dissenters, so widespread, in fact, that to ensure ratification of the Constitution in Virginia Madison agreed to press for a Bill of Rights as the first order of business in a newly elected Congress. The Constitution won ratification in 1788; Madison won election to the first House of Representatives in 1789; in that same year a Bill of Rights won congressional approval and had by 1791 won the approval of a sufficient number of states to become the first ten amendments to the Constitution. (For the evolution of the First Amendment, see Appendix A.)

As befitted Jefferson's concern when he named religious freedom first, the very first phrase of the First Amendment dealt with religion: "Congress shall make no law respecting an establishment of religion, or prohibiting the free exercise thereof." With a breathtaking economy of words, the Constitution now provided a double guarantee: first, that Congress shall do nothing to favor, promote, or endow religion; second, that Congress shall take no step that would impede, obstruct, or penalize religion. Neither hindering nor helping, government would simply leave religion alone. And religious persons, no matter how zealous or idiosyncratic their beliefs, had nothing to fear from government, nor did irreligious persons, no matter how heretical or scandalous their opinions. Once again, however, words were insufficient unless fully understood and faithfully applied. Both Jefferson and Madison throughout the remainder of their lives, in office and out, endeavored to give those sixteen words the soundest, sternest construction that they could bear. In 1791 Jefferson, at forty-eight years of age, and Madison, at forty, found the fight for religious freedom far from over.

In 1800 when John Adams and Thomas Jefferson engaged in the first wide open presidential campaign in American history, Jefferson's political enemies seized the occasion to abuse and condemn him for being opposed to religion. Anyone, they argued, could appear the champion of religious freedom if to such a person religion mattered little. Jefferson was the atheist, the infidel, the archdemon. He opposed biblical revelation and undermined Christian morals. He concealed his hostility to religion by talking only of its liberty. Anyone who says that it makes no difference whether one believes in twenty gods or no god cannot be counted a friend to Christianity and certainly ought not to be elected president of the United States. The price of Jefferson's battle for religious liberty might prove to be high indeed, threatening perhaps even his opportunity to become president. Jefferson was elected, however, though by no particularly comfortable margin: seventy-three electoral votes for him as opposed to sixty-five for John Adams.

Once president, Jefferson retreated in no way from his single-minded dedication to religious liberty. On the contrary, he wished to make clear that though not hostile to religion he was implacably hostile to any governmental meddling in religion. In his view, presidents should have nothing to do with thanksgiving proclamations or days of prayer or times of devotion. These were religious matters falling into the exclusive province of religious, not political, leaders; the right to issue such proclamations belonged strictly to the former, Jefferson declared, "and this right can never be safer than in their own hands, where the Constitution has deposited it."[15] In the very first year of his presidency, Jefferson seized the opportunity to stamp the First Amendment with his own understanding of its true meaning; moreover, he did so with a vigor and effect that brought his words and his sentiments forcefully into the nation's judicial history. Soon after his election in 1800 a group of Baptists in Danbury, Connecticut—Jefferson supporters all—wrote to express their appreciation for his election. In addition they asked Jefferson to set aside a day of fasting so that the nation might more readily heal the wounds of a bitterly divisive campaign.

Jefferson was, of course, unwilling to set aside such a day, with its clear religious overtones. He was also unwilling, however, to let pass the opportunity to make his point regarding governmental meddling, especially since he could make it to a group already warmly disposed toward him. Knowing that his response would give "great offence to the New England clergy" (i.e., Congregationalists—Federalists all), he nonetheless thought it necessary to explain why he, unlike Washington or Adams, would adopt a different stance with respect to officially sponsored religious observances. So his letter of reply (January 1, 1802) included this long and significant sentence:

Believing with you that religion is a matter which lies solely between man and his God, that he owes to none other for his faith or his worship, that the legislative powers of government reach actions only, and not opinions, I contemplate with solemn reverence that act of the whole American people which declared that their legislature should "make no law respecting an establishment of religion, or prohibiting the free exercise thereof," thus building a wall of separation between Church and State.[16]

Unconsciously echoing the language of Roger Williams, Jefferson found in the religion phrases of the First Amendment no vague or fuzzy language to be bent or shaped or twisted as suited any Supreme Court justice or White House incumbent. That amendment had built a wall, with the ecclesiastical estate on one side and the civil estate on the other. Jefferson first employed the metaphor, then endeavored for the rest of his life to give that metaphor as much brick and mortar as he possibly could.

So much is Jefferson identified in the American mind with his battle for political liberty that it is difficult to entertain the possibility that he felt even more strongly about religious liberty. If the letters and activities of his post presidential years can be taken as a fair guide, however, he maintained an unrelenting vigilance with respect to freedom in religion, and an unrelenting, perhaps even unforgiving, distrust of all those who would seek in any way to mitigate or limit or nullify that freedom. Something of Jefferson's rhetorical vigor is revealed in his 1810 letter to the botanist William Baldwin. A favorite theme of Jefferson's (to which we shall return in chapter 5) was the corruption of the pure religion of Jesus by those who carried on his name. But in elaborating his variations on that theme, Jefferson revealed his opinion of those who had perverted Christianity "into an engine for enslaving mankind." Across the ages, clergy have been interested not in truth but only in wealth and power; when rational people have had difficulty swallowing "their impious heresies," then the clergy have, with the help of the state, forced "them down their throats."[17] Five years later, he wrote of "this loathsome combination of church and state" that for so many centuries reduced human beings to "dupes and drudges."[18]

In 1816 Jefferson worried that, whatever the laws and the constitutional guarantees, the mood of the public could itself create a kind of inquisition. One reason that Jefferson declined to respond to questions about his own religion was that such responses might give the impression that the questioner had a right to know. And he did not! My religious opinions are my own, Jefferson repeatedly asserted, and sometimes silence is the only way to deal with those who would take away my right to think for myself, just as on other occasions "ridicule is the only weapon which can be used against unintelligible propositions."[19]

Near the end of his life, Jefferson gave himself to a final passion: the building of the University of Virginia. Here, too, his fervor for religious liberty was fully evident; indeed, it was this fervor that prevented any accommodation with the College of William and Mary. Otherwise, that college could have been transformed into *the* university for the state. Jefferson was willing to elevate his alma mater into new significance if it would move toward the population center of the state and if it would sever its Anglican, now Episcopal, ties. The college was prepared to negotiate on the former condition, but not on the latter. Jefferson, convinced that sectarian education placed major restraints upon that mind that "Almighty God hath made free," turned therefore to the planning and construction of an entirely new university, which, as he told Joseph Priestley, would be "broad & liberal & modern."[20] That meant, in Jefferson's view, that the university must be as free of denominational and clerical influence as he could make it. He would appoint professors in language and law, history and mathematics, natural philosophy and moral philosophy, but none in theology. Theology was no aid either to reason or education—rather, nothing other than a stumbling block and hindrance to both.

In 1820 as he described his plans for the University of Virginia to his former private secretary, William Short, Jefferson acknowledged that his plan for the first truly secular university would have opposition: weak opposition (in his view) from the College of William and Mary, but strong opposition from "the priests of the different religious sects, to whose spells on the human mind its improvement is ominous." They object to the appointment of anyone who is not an orthodox Trinitarian, and though the denominations are often at each other's throats on other matters, they unite in opposition to every step taken in the direction of a genuinely modern university. "The Presbyterian clergy are loudest, the most intolerant of all sects, the most tyrannical and ambitious; ready at the word of the lawgiver, if such a word could be now obtained, to put the torch to the pile, and to rekindle in this virgin hemisphere, the flames in which their oracle Calvin consumed the poor Servetus."[21]

Jefferson bemoaned the pattern of church life that gave the unenlightened and bigoted clergy "stated and privileged days to collect and catechize us, opportunities of delivering their oracles to the people in mass, and of moulding their minds as wax in the hollow of their hands." Despite this enormous advantage, however, Virginians are liberal enough, reasonable enough, to "give fair play" to a university set free from dogmatisms and fixed ideas.[22] Before the Revolution, Anglicans most worried Jefferson, for they had, or seemed to have, the greatest amount of priestly power in Virginia. After that War of Independence, Presbyterians assumed in Jefferson's mind this cloak of authority. (A large degree of Presbyterian influence in the state universities of both North and South Carolina may account in part for Jefferson's concern and bombast.) All efforts to control the mind require vigilant resistance. "If the freedom of religion, guaranteed to us by law in *theory*, can ever rise in *practice* under the overbearing inquisition of public opinion," then and only then will truth "prevail over fanaticism."[23]

If in his later years Jefferson worried more about priestly power in his own state, he never lost sight of the persisting force of the Congregational clergy in New England. They have gotten "a smell of union between church and state," Jefferson wrote in 1801, and it would be difficult for them to get that out of their system.[24] He rejoiced with John Adams when the Congregational church was finally disestablished in Connecticut in 1818; welcoming "the resurrection of Connecticut to light and liberty," Jefferson congratulated Adams "that this den of priesthood is at length broken up, and that a protestant popedom is no longer to disgrace American history and character."[25] Earlier he had written to the governor of New Hampshire in the hope that Dartmouth College could be legally changed from a small sectarian college to a genuinely public university, no longer the exclusive domain of an elite Congregationalism. "Our lawyers and our priests," he wrote, "suppose that preceding generations held the earth more freely than we do" and that they can make laws and establish trusts that cannot be altered, "even to make them answer their end." In short, they believe that "the earth belongs to the dead, and not to the living." In 1819 the famous Dartmouth case was decided in favor of the school's founders, the issue going the way of Federalists John Marshall and Daniel Webster, not the way of Republican Jefferson.[26]

The most famous Jeffersonian phrase concerning liberty, carved on his monument in Washington and engraved on the minds of all libertarians, is this: "For I have sworn upon the altar of god, eternal hostility against every form of tyranny over the mind of man." But, one asks, What does this have to do with religious liberty? There lies the irony, for this Jeffersonian cry of the heart sprang wholly from his passionate concern for this "first liberty." In a letter in 1800 to a physician and friend, Benjamin Rush, Jefferson admitted that the clergy ("the genus *irritabile vatum*," the irritable tribe of priests) were "all in arms" against him. Despite the First Amendment, they continued to hope that establishment might come to their own particular denomination, and especially was this true of the Episcopalians and the Congregationalists. And they oppose my candidacy for President, because "they believe that any portion of power confided to me will be exerted in opposition to their schemes. And they believe truly." Then follows immediately the famous sentence just quoted: "For I have sworn upon the altar of god, eternal hostility against every form of tyranny over the mind of man."[27] For Jefferson, the oldest and bloodiest and most deeply entrenched form of such tyranny had been in the name of religion; he, therefore, would in this arena never drop his guard, never allow his gaze to wander or his rhetoric to soften. Almighty God had made the mind free; in the name of God, it must be kept free.

A presidential James Madison during his years in office (1809–17), like a presidential Thomas Jefferson, labored to make clear what a "Memorial and Remonstrance" of 1785, a Virginia Statute of 1786, and a First Amendment of 1791 were all about. An opportunity presented itself to Madison in 1811 when he found a congressional bill on his desk entitled An Act incorporating the Protestant Episcopal Church in the town of Alexandria, in the District of Columbia. Such a bill, first of all, raised many memories of the Episcopal church's effort to be incorporated by the state legislature of Virginia soon after the Revolution was won. If any church other than the old established one had sought incorporation, the issue could have been treated with some objectivity and dispassion. But here was England's church, now abruptly disestablished, trying to insinuate itself back into some position of favor and privilege—or so many citizens of Virginia believed. The Episcopal church had briefly gained the right to incorporate in 1784, but in the wake of the "Memorial and Remonstrance," as well as the Jefferson Statute, the House of Delegates in December 1786 repealed that act under which incorporation had been granted. By the following January this repeal had become Virginia law.[28] Clearly, any suggestion of a return to *status quo ante* in the realm of religion would be strenuously and successfully resisted.

Madison, naturally aware of all this history and of all the passions pertaining thereto, viewed with grave skepticism this new endeavor by the Episcopal church to be incorporated in the District of Columbia, such incorporation to be achieved through an act of the United States Congress. In Madison's view, this congressional action flew directly in the face of the First Amendment; as he pointed out in his veto message (February 21, 1811), such a bill blurred, if it did not erase, "the essential distinction between civil and religious function." The bill "enacts into and establishes by law," Madison continued, "sundry rules and proceedings" that pertain purely to the operation of the Episcopal church. The effect, therefore, "would so far be a religious establishment by law" of this particular institution. Moreover, the bill followed the old Virginia pattern of having the church operate as the agency for charity and the education of the poor. This, Madison stated, "would be a precedent for giving to religious societies as such a legal agency in carrying into effect a public and civil duty."[29] One week later, Madison vetoed a bill that would have provided federal land to a Baptist church in the Mississippi Territory. Such action, Madison noted, "comprises a precedent for the appropriation of funds of the United States for the use and support of religious societies," and that quite simply, quite firmly, violated the First Amendment.

Sometime after he left the presidency, Madison wrote what have come to be known as the "Detached Memoranda," these notes offering recollections of Franklin and Washington as well as reflections on major public questions. Some of those reflections pertained to religion, or what Madison called "ecclesiastical endowments," as he grouped churches with his discussion of monopolies and corporations. He also recalled the two vetoes noted above, seeing them as measures designed to resist those subtle steps by which the First Amendment might become a nullity. In the United States not enough attention was given, not enough vigilance was exercised, with respect to what Madison called "the silent accumulations and encroachments by Ecclesiastical Bodies."

With pardonable pride, he pointed to Virginia's having early taken the boldest strides in behalf of religious liberty. He recalled the efforts of Patrick Henry to promote a general assessment bill; it was "supported by all his eloquence, aided by the remaining prejudices of the Sect which before the Revolution had been established by law." But in a matter of such moment many insisted that all the people be given a chance to express their views. And so they did—in overwhelming opposition, as Madison remembered with pleasure. The "Memorial and Remonstrance," he wrote now in retirement, "met with the approbation of the Baptists, the Presbyterians, the Quakers, and the few Roman Catholics, universally; of the Methodists in part; and even of not a few of the Sect formerly established by law." When Patrick Henry's bill was defeated and Jefferson's passed in its stead, the effect, Madison asserted, was to erect the "true standard of Religious liberty: its principle the great barrier against usurpations on the rights of conscience."[30]

Yet many states lacked language that compelling, that distinct. They, therefore, must be especially watchful, Madison warned, for those "silent accumulations & encroachments." What Madison chiefly had in mind (and this explains the context of monopolies and corporations) was "the indefinite accumulation of property from the capacity of holding it in perpetuity." Look at Great Britain and most of Europe, Madison advised, to see what horrendous problems had been created where the Church sometimes owned as much as half the property of the nation. This fact "promoted if not caused" the Reformation, which should have been lesson enough to all the Western world. But, Madison cautioned, it can all happen again.

In particular, Madison asked whether or not his fellow citizens were "duly awake to the tendency of the precedents they are establishing, in the multiplied incorporations [that issue again!] of Religious Congregations with the faculty of acquiring & holding property real as well as personal?" Most acts of incorporation set no limits of time or amount. Consider, therefore: "Must not bodies, perpetual in their existence, and which may be always gaining without ever losing, speedily gain more than is useful, and in time more than is safe?" Land values in America were increasing rapidly, and additional gifts made for enormous wealth. Let us remember, the patriarchal Madison advised, that "the people of the U. S. owe their Independence & their liberty to the wisdom of descrying in the minute tax of 3 pence on tea, the magnitude of the evil comprized in the precedent. Let them exert the same wisdom in watching ag[ain]st every evil lurking under plausible disguises and growing up from small beginnings."[31] Forty years earlier, a persuasive and logical Madison had made his case convincingly before a Virginia legislature; now, with similar logic and matured wisdom Madison sought to make his case before a whole nation: Remember your history, value your liberty, and stand by those principles in which you believe! What does it matter that the tax on tea was a mere three pence per pound? A principle was at stake. What does it matter that the land on which a Baptist church stood was worth only a few dollars? A principle was at stake.

And so Madison moved to another issue that most Americans in the 1820s (or the 1980s) worried about very little. In the 1820s this issue struck many as picayune, a trifle, a nonissue—but not to Madison. Here was his innocent question: "Is the appointment of Chaplains to the two Houses of Congress consistent with the Constitution, and with the pure principle of religious freedom?" An innocent question, perhaps, but few could doubt what Madison's answer would be.

The establishment of the chaplainship to Cong[res]s is a palpable violation of equal rights, as well as of Constitutional principles. The tenets of the chaplains elected [by the majority] shut the door of worship ag[ain]st the members whose creeds & consciences forbid a participation in that of the majority. To say nothing of other sects, this is the case with that of Roman Catholics & Quakers who have always had members in one or both of the Legislative branches. Could a Catholic clergyman ever hope to be appointed a Chaplain? To say that his religious principles are obnoxious or that his sect is small, is to lift the evil at once and exhibit in its naked deformity the doctrine that religious truth is to be tested by numbers, or that the major sects have a right to govern the minor.[32]

Religion, after all, must be a voluntary act, and if congressmen believe they must have the benefit of clergy, then let them do as all other citizens do, as their own constituents do: voluntarily contribute to the support of their chaplains. If the public is obliged to provide religious services for the legislative branch, then why not for the executive and judicial as well? (That rhetorical question sounded more rhetorical in the early nineteenth century than in the late twentieth.) To the modern riposte that we should pay for these chaplains because congressmen need all the help they can get, Madison already had the answer many decades ago. Few bother to attend the services of these "legal Ecclesiastics," and the whole exercise has become "a tiresome formality."[33]

But Madison was not through shocking his public with his strict libertarianism in religion. Chaplains even for the army and the navy ought to be avoided. Oh I know, Madison said in effect; arguments to the contrary are most persuasive. Nevertheless, what we are doing is establishing religion, and it is a religion mixed with political and military authority. "The object of this establishment is seducing; the motive to it is laudable." Yet, let us remember we do have a Constitution. "Is it not safer to adhere to a right principle, and trust to its consequences, than confide in the reasoning however [alluring] in favor of a wrong one?" Madison conceded that arguments against his position could be especially strong when troops were far away or isolated from ordinary means of religious counsel and succor. Nevertheless—always that "nevertheless"—Madison could not divorce himself from the general truth "that it is safer to trust the consequences of a right principle than reasonings in support of a bad one."[34]

As president, James Madison faced the same dilemma that con-

fronted Thomas Jefferson: that is, the matter of executive proclamations in language that might be religious and for purposes that
might also be religious. Jefferson solved the problem by simply
refusing to issue any such proclamations. Madison was disposed
to follow that same pattern, but an American public—denied any
high priest for eight long years—was restive. When the War of
1812 was declared, Congress passed a resolution requesting the
president to issue a proclamation. On the one hand, related as this
request was to "his" unpopular war, Madison felt he could not
ignore the resolution; on the other hand, he firmly believed it no
legitimate part of the duty of civil government to set aside religious days. He compromised by issuing a proclamation as utterly
nonsectarian as he could make it ("absolutely indiscriminate"),
and by ensuring that it carried not the slightest hint of penalty for
failure to comply ("merely recommendatory").[35] But the whole
exercise struck Madison as something that presidents of these
United States simply ought not to be involved in. Having found
himself in this awkward role, Madison now offered five reasons
why religious or quasi-religious pronouncements should not be
handed down from on high—why presidents should not be popes.

First, a declaration of a religious day of fasting or feasting or
praying can never be anything but a mere recommendation, and
"an *advisory* Govt is a contradiction in terms." Second, neither the
legislative nor the executive branch can in any sense regard itself
as an ecclesiastical council or synod, with authority to address "the
faith or the Consciences of the people." Third, such proclamations
"seem to imply and certainly nourish the erroneous idea of a
national religion." Here again, Madison wondered if the American
people were yet ready to take the idea of disestablishment seriously. Even if we were all of the same denomination and the same
creed, any "universal act of religion . . . . ought to be effected thro'
the intervention of" the religious and not the political authorities.
But since we are not all of the same church, such national action
by political leaders is "doubly wrong." Fourth, such proclamations
tended to employ the language and theology of the dominant
group or groups, with the consequent tendency that a conformity

to the religious viewpoints of the majority would be surreptitiously encouraged. Fifth and last, such proclamations inescapably bent religious principles to political expediency. Religion became a matter of party politics, however great the effort to avoid that sad result.[36] In sum, James Madison found any encouragement of "national religion" to be illegal or inequitable or frightening.

In letters written in his retirement at Montpelier, Madison, like Jefferson, continued to believe that separation of church and state was best both for the church and for the state. Prior to the American experiment, he wrote in 1819, "it was the universal opinion . . . that civil Government could not stand without the prop of a religious establishment, and that the Christian religion itself would perish if not supported by a legal provision for its clergy." That universal opinion has now been disproved, by Virginia at the state level as well as by America at the federal level.[37] In some parts of the country, however, "there remains . . . a strong bias towards the old error, that without some sort of alliance or coalition between Govt & Religion neither can be duly supported." So strong was this bias, this tendency to revert, that "the danger cannot be too carefully guarded ag[ain]st." The only ultimate protection for religious liberty in a country like ours, Madison pointed out—echoing Jefferson—is public opinion: a firm and pervading opinion that the First Amendment works. "Every new & successful example therefore of a perfect separation between ecclesiastical and civil matters, is of importance."[38] In 1822 when this last letter was written, Madison did not believe that the evidence was all in or that the books could be safely closed. More than a century and a half later, that evidence is still not all in, nor can the books be safely closed today.

Madison was far more interested in talking about the limits within which religious institutions should operate than about the truths that religious scholarship might uncover. Notoriously reticent about his own beliefs, Madison (unlike Jefferson) left the subject of religious truth largely to others. Trained under John Witherspoon at Princeton in Scottish realism, well read in the rational apologetics of the Anglican Samuel Clarke, self-tutored for a time after his graduation in biblical and other religious materials, Madison was certainly no religious illiterate. With his mental agility and excellent education, Madison could have been a distinguished theologian. He chose, however, another route. Although theology may have continued to hold some fascination for him, little evidence from his own pen justifies such a conclusion.

In a well-known letter written to the Episcopal clergyman Frederick Beasley in 1825, Madison responded to a request for his views of a tract dealing with the being and attributes of God. Madison was polite, but noncommital, quick to admit that in such matters he swiftly moved beyond his depth. He confessed to having read Clarke on this subject—but "fifty years ago only," apparently never to return to that or similar apologetic volumes. Agreeing that belief in an all-powerful, all-wise God "is essential to the moral order of the World & to the happiness of man" and that all arguments to establish the existence of such a God should be as coherent as possible, Madison failed to declare what he believed about such a God. He acknowledged that finite human understanding found more comfort or "more facility" in positing the existence of such a Causal Being than in facing only "an infinite series of cause & effect," but Madison failed once again to indicate what gave comfort to his understanding. What captured Madison's energies, abilities, and time was not what truths lay at the end of the religious quest but the right of all humankind to seek those truths without penalty or burden or any civil disability whatsoever.[39]

We do not praise Madison faintly to acclaim him chiefly for his lifelong dedication to the cause of religious liberty. In that famous "Memorial," Madison penned a line found useful to the United States Supreme Court over and over. The line reads: "It is proper to take alarm at the first experiment on our liberties." That "prudent jealousy," Madison added, was one of the "noblest characteristics of the late Revolution." Opponents to the Stamp Act and patriots at the Tea Party took alarm while time remained to do something about the threat to liberty. These words of Madison, like the "eternal hostility" words of Jefferson, are well known and widely quoted. But again, these words of Madison, like those of Jefferson, are often so far removed from their original context that Americans tend to forget what provoked the initial passion in the breast of each man. What provoked their passion and sustained their vigilance was *religious* liberty: winning it, watching over it, preserving it—everywhere and for all time. Almighty God has made the mind free. . . .

4. The Icons: Franklin and Washington

The last decade of the eighteenth century found Americans searching for a center. Once that center had been located in loyalty to England and to the monarchy, but this loyalty could no longer unify. Later that center had been the military effort required to overthrow Britain's army and navy, but the Revolution had now ended. True, a new Constitution had been drawn up, presented to the people and, with much grumbling and opposition, ratified— often by the narrowest of margins. In such political transition or even turmoil, a body of citizens might turn for strength, comfort, and solidarity to a single pervading church that stood firm above all changes of political allegiance and all crises of war and peace. But Americans had no such national church. What symbolic center drew Americans, qua Americans, together? What oneness could be found? What forces, if any, held together thirteen suspicious states and three million uncertain people? In so delicate and anxious a time, hope for unity centered chiefly on two national heroes: Benjamin Franklin (1706–1790) and George Washington (1732–1799)—and both men died in the very first decade of this very new nation. O Israel, Israel, "Hear the word of the Lord . . . for the Lord has a controversy with the inhabitants of the land"[1]—or so it seemed in those troubled and vulnerable years.

A few years before Franklin's death in 1790, a group of citizens in Massachusetts determined to name their town after the Philadelphia oracle and sage. Proposing to add a steeple to their meetinghouse, they suggested to Franklin that he might wish to donate a bell to hang therein. The ever-practical Franklin, honored to have New Englanders favor him in this fashion, responded that they should spare themselves the expense of a steeple and that, instead of a bell, he would send them a gift of books, "Sense being preferable to Sound" in any case. Such books would serve as a beginning for a parish library "for the Use of a Society of intelligent, respectable Farmers, such as our Country People generally consist of." When the parish minister, Nathaniel Emmons, preached a sermon in honor of the Franklin bounty, he entitled it "The Dignity of Man: A Discourse addressed to the Congregation in Franklin upon the Occasion of their receiving from Dr. Franklin the Mark of his Respect in a rich Donation of Books . . ." And when the sermon was printed, it included this dedication: "To his Excellency Benjamin Franklin, President of the State of Pennsylvania, the Ornament of Genius, the Patron of Science, and the Boast of Man."[2]

Emmons chose as his text for the occasion the charge of David to Solomon that he "Show thyself a man."[3] Solomon turned out to be a "Boast of Man," as, indeed, did Franklin. And though his contemporaries did not commonly compare Franklin to biblical heroes, the Solomon analogy has considerable merit—especially if we allow ourselves to think of the traditional Solomon, author of the Book of Proverbs, the Song of Solomon, even the Wisdom of Solomon. "Solomon in all his glory" is the Solomon to be held in view as we consider Franklin in all his glory, both in life and, even more, in death.

Franklin of *Poor Richard's Almanac* is reminiscent of the Solomon of Proverbs, partly, no doubt, because Franklin was willing to borrow wise sayings from wherever he might find them. Many of the canonical proverbs have a practicality, a homeyness, a secularity, not far removed from the widely read, widely repeated sayings of Poor Richard. "Love your neighbor," Franklin advised, "yet don't pull down your hedge." "Friendship cannot live with ceremony or without civility." "He that falls in love with himself will have no rivals." "Nothing brings more pain than too much pleasure; nothing more bondage than too much liberty." Some of Franklin's observations have not lost their power to amuse: "Keep your eyes wide open before marriage, and half shut afterwards" and "Here my poor Bridget's corpse doth lie,/She is at rest, and so am I." In the realm of religion, practicality supplanted theory: "Many have quarreled about religion that never practiced it" and "Serving God is doing good to man, but praying is thought an easier service and therefore is more generally chosen."[4] Franklin, who won his first public through the proverbs, found in them and the *Almanac* sufficient profit to enable him to retire from the printing business at the age of forty-two. He could then allow his insatiable curiosity, his wide-ranging experimental playfulness, to carry him where they would.

A familiar facet of the traditional Solomon's wisdom is reflected in that famous decision between two women claiming to be the mother of the same child. Franklin again and again found himself likewise balancing claims of contesting parties, his general posture being one of searching for a reasonable compromise, a sensible solution, an escape through the horns of a dilemma. Many of his services as arbitrator and diplomat took place in the political arena, and on these much of his fame rests. But on a surprising number of occasions he also sought to be a Solomon in the religious arena. Though himself surely a freethinker, Franklin cautioned other freethinkers to be careful about dismissing institutional religion too lightly or too quickly. "Think how great a proportion of Mankind," he warned in 1757, "consists of weak and ignorant Men and Women, and of inexperienc'd Youth of both Sexes, who have need of the Motives of Religion to restrain them from Vice, to support their Virtue, and retain them in the Practice of it till it becomes *habitual,* which is the great Point for its Security."[5] So institutional religion should not be discarded—even though it may need to be restrained. Why is it that church people have so little charity, so little tolerance for those beyond their own narrow fold? "We zealous Presbyterians," he wrote his sister in 1760, are "too apt to think ourselves alone in the right." "Besides all the Heathens, Mahometans and Papists, whom we give to Satan in a Lump, other Sects of Christian Protestants that do not agree with us, will hardly escape Perdition."[6]

When Franklin was in London serving as colonial agent for Pennsylvania (and other colonies as well), he played the role of conciliator and mediator between Britain and its North American people almost too well, being seen for a while as unsympathetic to those whom he presumably represented. But Franklin disdained making too much of issues not crucial. The desire of some Anglicans for a bishop to be sent to America was, in his view, one such hullabaloo without much substance. "I cannot think it a matter of such Moment," he wrote his sister in 1769, "as to be a sufficient Reason for Division among you." I don't believe, he added, that having a bishop in America "would either be of such Advantage to Episcopalians, or such Disadvantage to Anti-episcopalians as either seems to imagine." After cautioning against religious squabbles in general, he concluded with a typical Franklin touch: "Indeed when religious People quarrel about Religion, or hungry People about their Victuals, it looks as if they had not much of either among them."[7] People get terribly worked up about Arianism or Socinianism, when the only "ism" that troubled him, he reported with a straight face, was rheumatism.[8]

Franklin did not turn aside everything with a witticism, though a story made the rounds that he was not asked to write the Declaration of Independence because everyone was convinced he would try to hide a joke in there somewhere. Back in this country when the Revolution broke out, Franklin in Pennsylvania faced the very serious problem of conscientious objection on a wide scale: Quakers, of course, but also Mennonites, Moravians, Schwenkfelders, and others. What to do in this situation, when every able-bodied man was needed, when no group could be excused? On the one hand, how can we treat sensitive religious consciences with liberality and justice? On the other hand, how can we place all the burden for waging and winning a war against mighty England on the remaining segments of Pennsylvania's population? Here one needed the wisdom of Solomon!

In private correspondence Franklin advised a Moravian friend to at least give young men some military training and to provide arms to those willing to use them. If the Moravians would only say that they compelled no one to use arms, but did not "restrain such as are disposed," that, said Franklin, would "operate in the Minds of the People very greatly in your Favour."[9] More formally, Franklin drafted proposals that he hoped conscientious objectors would be willing to sign. If they would sign, two vital consequences would follow: opposition to Britain would be greater, and opposition from their neighbors would be less. Franklin's proposals were specific: religious pacifists would agree to help put out fires in cities or towns; would help evacuate women and children, the old and infirm, from places under attack; would help dig trenches or fortifications for defense; and, with litters, would carry "off wounded Men to places where they may receive Assistance."[10] The Assembly in its final action was not as generous as Franklin had tried to be, for that body demanded payment of taxes as well as rendering of voluntary efforts in behalf of the Revolution. But from all this Franklin emerges as the wise and tolerant statesman, sensitive to religious conscience, trying to keep neighbors from each other's throats when a far more urgent battle needed to be fought.

Franklin also sought conciliation and mediation, most of his life, on that well-trampled battleground of theology. The one exception to his moderate tone was when, as a mere youth of eighteen, Franklin found himself already exasperated by metaphysical niceties and theological subtleties. In a *Dissertation on Liberty and Necessity* (1725) the brash and impudent young man demonstrated that in this world there is much necessity, hardly any liberty, and virtually no point to religion. He printed only a few copies of this small tract, burned many of these, and later described this booklet as one of the "errata" of his life. His far more familiar stance was one of genial tolerance with respect to doctrine, arguing only that good works constituted the finest evidence of good beliefs. Franklin became involved in the notorious affair of the Irish Presbyterian minister Samuel Hemphill in 1735 for many reasons, but high among them was Franklin's conviction that this clergyman placed a proper emphasis on moral truths rather than leading his congregation into a theological swamp. "Zealous Presbyterians," on the other hand, wanted more doctrinal orthodoxy as well as more evangelical passion. Franklin already had his fill of dogma from the senior minister, Jedidiah Andrews, who seemed interested only in making good Presbyterians instead of good citizens; his sermons, said Franklin, "were all to me very dry, uninteresting and unedifying, since not a single moral Principle was inculcated or enforc'd."[11]

In a satirizing "Dialogue between Two Presbyterians," Franklin made his point that faith without works is not only dead, it smells bad. "Morality or Virtue is the End," Franklin's spokesman asserted, with faith "only a Means to obtain that End." Hemphill was charged with heresy because he spent so little time trying to bring men and women to Christ. But "upon a supposition that we all have Faith in Christ already, as I think we have, where can be the Damage of being exhorted to Good Works? Is Virtue Heresy; and Universal Benevolence False Doctrine, that any of us should keep away from Meeting because it is preached there?"[12] Well, of course, the long and unsavory dispute was more complicated than that, but in the end it was Franklin who decided to "keep away from Meeting." Nothing in the Hemphill affair gave him grounds for thinking that theological disputes were profitable, or even meaningful.

The philosopher David Hume and Franklin exchanged letters about a troublesome controversy in Prussia in the 1760s concerning the duration of punishment and torment in hell. Eternity seemed to cover such a terribly long time that Hume advised the local governor to use his influence to shorten the sentence of the damned. And Scotland's Hume indicated that America's Franklin shared his sentiment. In reply to Hume, Franklin said that the Prussian wrangle reminded him of a Puritan dispute about a maypole: some citizens wanting one, others opposing. The mayor, beseiged by both sides, finally rendered his judicious verdict: "You that are for having no Maypole shall have no Maypole; and you that are for having a Maypole shall have a Maypole. Get about your business and let me hear no more of this Quarrel." So, said Franklin, with tongue firmly in cheek, I think we might similarly deal with this troublesome doctrine of eternal torment in hell. Let this be our decision: "You that are for no more Damnation than is proportion'd to your Offences, have my Consent that it may be so: And you that are for being damn'd eternally, G—d eternally d——n you all, and let me hear no more of your Disputes."[13] For this "zealous Presbyterian," doctrine must never become the end in itself, nor should it ever be the instrument by which life is impoverished rather than enriched. Sounding very much like John Adams, Franklin observed in a 1760 letter: "For there is no Rank in Natural Knowledge of equal Dignity and Importance with that of being a good Parent, a good Child, a good Husband, or Wife, a good Neighbour or Friend, a good Subject or citizen, that is, in short, a good Christian."[14]

To Samuel Mather in 1773 Franklin confessed that theology was not really his keenest concern; it is "rather more out of my Walk."[15] And to another correspondent in 1779 Franklin announced that metaphysics disgusted him at a very early age, so much so "that I quitted that kind of reading and study for others more satisfactory."[16] When writing to London's famous Unitarian preacher Richard Price, Franklin chose not to "wade any deeper in Theology," knowing that he would soon be "out of my Depth."[17] But Franklin's good friend Ezra Stiles of Yale could press the wise old oracle harder than most, and like all oracles, Franklin could respond with studied ambiguity. Stiles asked Franklin directly and boldly, but not (Stiles assured his friend) from the "Impertinence of improper Curiosity," for a more straightforward and explicit statement of his Christian convictions. Somewhat taken aback, Franklin reported that this was the "first time I have been questioned upon it." Nonetheless, the eighty-three-year-old deist indicated that he took no offense and therefore responded on March 9, 1790—only five weeks before his death—as follows:

Here is my Creed. I believe in one God, Creator of the Universe: That he governs the World by his Providence. That he ought to be worshipped. That the most acceptable Service we can render to him, is doing good to his other Children. That the Soul of Man is immortal, and will be treated with Justice in another Life, respect[ing] its Conduct in this. These I take to be the fundamental Principles of all sound Religion, and I regard them as you do, in whatever Sect I meet with them.[18]

But Stiles wanted to know particularly what Franklin thought of Jesus. Was Franklin, after all, really a Christian or not? Franklin responded that Jesus had given to the world the best system of morals and religion that "the World ever saw," but that unfortunately that system had "received various corrupting changes." With respect to the divinity of Jesus, "I have, with most of the present Dissenters in Engl[an]d, some Doubts . . . tho' it is a Question I do not dogmatize upon, hav[ing] never studied it, & think it needless to busy myself with it now, when I expect soon an Opport[unity] of know[ing] the Truth with less Trouble."[19] Had he ever been brought to a heresy trial, the parrying Franklin would have proved a slippery witness indeed.

America's wise Solomon won his reputation for wisdom—world-wide—mainly, of course, as scientist and inventor. "Dr." Franklin had honorary degrees conferred upon him by every college in this country when his discoveries in electricity were publicized early in the 1750s. He was elected to the Royal Academy in Paris and to the Royal Society in London, this primitive backwoodsman who was just fooling around with his Leyden jars, glass rods, and "batteries." Franklin not only turned the fascination with electricity from a parlor game into a science, he invented most of the words still used today in connection with that startling phenomenon. And for Franklin, theory was meaningless if divorced from practice, this principle as true in science as in religion. So "Franklin's points," or the lightning rods, delivered an age from the fear and calamity of fire even as they substituted the daylight of reason for the darkness of superstition. But Franklin never stopped inventing, discovering, investigating, and creating: the Franklin stove and the Franklin bifocals, the relationship between heat and the color of clothing, the relevance of the Gulf Stream to transatlantic navigation, the connections between tides and rivers, between sunspots and storms. He founded fire companies and libraries, endorsed aerial observation and navigation, promoted a more efficient postal system, and even fathered the notion of daylight savings time. What wisdom and what genius could Americans point to with both affection and pride of ownership! America's

Solomon he was, and if the queen of Sheba did not come to pay homage, so many others did arrive that her absence was scarcely noticed.

Franklin could compete with Solomon in proverbs and wise sayings; he could compete in wisdom and genius. When it comes to the erotic Song of Solomon, comparisons should perhaps not be pressed too far—though Franklin would not shy away from the contest. God created for us a world of delights, he wrote in his late twenties, and "I believe he is not offended when he sees his Children solace themselves in any manner of pleasant Exercises and innocent Delights."[20] Then, of course, Franklin's oft-quoted advice to a young man choosing a mistress displayed a worldliness and gentle cynicism altogether worthy of that earlier but hardly wiser Solomon.[21]

In the summer of 1785, Franklin returned from eight years in France, where he had rendered valuable service during the early years of the Revolution and even more valuable service in the later negotiations for peace. The darling of Paris, the returning diplomat found himself acclaimed even at home. Cannons boomed, bells rang, people thronged to welcome their very own Solomon home to Philadelphia. When the Constitution was drawn up two years later in his hometown, Franklin played no major role in the drafting of the document. But he was there, and that mere presence was enough to help win its approval, not just in Pennsylvania but up and down the entire Atlantic coast. From Massachusetts, Franklin's sister wrote: "It is not profanity to compare you to our Blessed Saviour who Employed much of his time while on Earth in doing good to the body's as well as souls of men & I am shure I think the comparison just."[22]

If such a comparison seemed strained in Franklin's lifetime, it appeared less so at his death. Franklin died in April 1790—less than a year after the Constitution had been ratified and George Washington elected. A tense moment—America stood poised, ready to take its first tentative steps toward nationhood or its first missteps toward disaster. What might strong central government mean to a tyranny-despising people? Would the nation descend into just another tyranny, distinguished from the earlier one only by being closer at hand and therefore harder to escape? What lay ahead in troubled relationships with England and with France? Would the several states find common interest or only pursue narrow and parochial ones? How could Solomon depart when his wisdom, his diplomacy, his genius were so desperately needed?

Thousands upon thousands turned out for Franklin's funeral on April 21, their anxiety mixed with their tributes and their sorrow. The following year a memorial service was held at the German Lutheran church in Franklin's city so that the whole nation could honor its now silent oracle. Those attending included President and Mrs. George Washington, Vice President and Mrs. John Adams, most of the United States senators and representatives, the corporate body of the American Philosophical Society (whose president Franklin had long been), and, of course, the local brotherhood of printers.

The Reverend Dr. William Smith, Anglican divine, College of Philadelphia provost, and frequent opponent of Franklin, delivered the lengthy eulogy. Not a time for stirring up old controversies or airing old grievances, this was a moment to bring the brand-new nation together, to heal, to "comfort ye, comfort ye, my people." It was time to raise up for veneration a national icon, a cultic hero, and this is precisely what Dr. Smith was prepared to do. He presented to his earnest listeners a New World luminary, an Old Testament patriarch, a classical world Hercules, lawgiver, philosopher, "splendid sun of science," statesman, and universal genius. In his peroration Smith himself rose to Olympian heights: "Let all thy fellow citizens; let all thy compatriots; let every class of men with whom thou wert associated here on earth . . . let them consider thee as their guardian-genius, still present and presiding amongst them; and what they conceive thou wouldst advise to be DONE, let them advise and DO likewise—and they shall not greatly deviate from the path of virtue and glory!"[23] One can only ask: If Franklin's enemies spoke this way, whatever would his friends say?

William Smith likely did not believe all that he had to say on this solemn occasion, but that is beside the point. The country needed to hear it said and needed to believe it. Cleansed of all doubt, purged of all anxiety, united in a clear and unambiguous loyalty to the now-buried Solomon, the new nation could gird up its loins and go forth into a world of watchful if not rapacious nations. Smith recognized the moment. "Circumstanced as the people of these United States now are," he declaimed, "in building up and completing the glorious fabric of American empire and happiness," we hold up Benjamin Franklin for your contemplation, your adoration, your emulation.[24] Smith acknowledged that these were not his sentiments alone. In preparing the eulogy, he had the help of such stalwarts as Benjamin Rush, David Rittenhouse, Thomas Jefferson, and others. But beyond that limited, literal sense in which Smith spoke for others, he spoke symbolically for a whole people—as did Jefferson when he acclaimed Franklin as "the greatest man and ornament of the age and country in which he lived . . . whose name will be like a star of the first magnitude in the firmament of heaven, when the memory of those who have surrounded and obscured him, will be lost in the abyss of time."[25] Solomon in all his glory . . .

What dazzling portraits these are, painted in brilliant rhetoric and rococo style! But the artists who used paint and canvas had not been idle either; indeed, well before Franklin's death, their contribution to Franklin as icon had begun. A Fragonard drawing, executed in 1778 and entitled *Dr. Franklin Crowned by Liberty*, revealed a bust of Franklin resting on a globe of the earth; he was attended by a cherub, while an ethereal female representing Liberty descended from the sun-drenched skies to place not one but two wreaths on Franklin's head. An even better known design of Fragonard's, etched by Marguerite Gerard, illustrated Turgot's famous epigram regarding Franklin: He seized fire from the heavens and the scepter from the tyrant's hand (see Figure 1). In this etching, Franklin ruled the cosmos, as lightning struck Minerva's shield (supported by Franklin) and Mars, at Franklin's direction, slew the figures of Tyranny and Avarice. A calm but clearly omnipotent Franklin commanded all the forces of heaven and earth.[26]

Figure 1

"Au Genie de Franklin," Margeurite Gerard (after Fragonard). Courtesy of Philadelphia Museum of Art: Mrs. John D. Rockefeller

In that same year of the Franco-American alliance (1788), Jean Charles Le Vasseur offered a line engraving (after a painting by Borel) that placed Franklin somewhat more firmly on earth, though he was again surrounded by the gods and goddesses of antiquity (see Figure 2). A contemporary advertisement in Paris described the work this way: "This drawing represents M. Franklin who liberated America: [An Indian maiden, symbolizing "Independent America,"] embraces the Statute of Liberty, & Minerva protects the wise legislator with her shell. Prudence & Courage overthrow their enemy who, in his fall, carries down Neptune, whose trident is broken. At the right of Liberty, Agriculture, Commerce and the Arts applaud the happy revolution."[27] For the French, particularly, Liberty was Franklin even as Franklin personified America.

Two decades after Franklin's death, an American artist in London, Benjamin West, presented his countrymen with an oil painting that won wide popularity (see Figure 3). *Franklin Drawing Electricity from the Sky* portrayed the philosopher-scientist seated on a rock, extending his right arm to the famous kite string and key, fire shooting out from the key. In Franklin's left hand may be seen the calculations that led him out from the crude laboratory visible in the corner. Surrounding cherubs add to the heavenly aura of this now totally mythologized event.[28] Franklin, no longer mortal, was like Elijah translated by the hand of God. And yet, as William Smith had affirmed, he was "present still and presiding amongst" us. He was here to guide, to inspire, to unite. He was the nation's icon or even, as his sister Jane Mecom dared to say, "our blessed Saviour." In 1749 Franklin had written of the "Necessity of a Publick Religion," a religion so called because of its evident usefulness to society. A generation later Franklin had himself become the cult object of just such a religion.[29]

A civil religion centered on Washington is a more familiar story, but that familiarity must not blind us to the urgency and the fervor that an untried nation invested in the elevation of Washington to

Figure 2

"L'Amerique Independant," Jean-Charles Le Vasseur (after Borel). Courtesy
of Philadelphia Museum of Art: Mrs. John D. Rockefeller

Figure 3

"Benjamin Franklin Drawing Electricity from the Sky," Benjamin West.
Courtesy of Philadelphia Museum of Art: Sinkler Collection

mythic status. Franklin was genius and mediator; Washington was creator and father. He caused the world, America's world, to be. In the waning weeks of the eighteenth century, George Washington caught a cold while inspecting his fields at Mount Vernon. In a few days, he was dead, passing from this life with the same controlled dignity with which he had lived. For Americans, a future without Washington was ominous, virtually inconceivable. About to enter a new century, the citizens of the United States made an unconscious, spontaneous decision: they would not let Washington go. He who held this nation together in his life would not be relieved of that responsibility even in death.

The enconiums heaped upon Washington knew no bounds. President John Adams declared a time of national mourning from his death in December 1799 to the following twenty-second of February. (When Franklin died, Jefferson had suggested to President Washington that a period of national mourning be set aside. Washington demurred on the ground that it was unwise to set such a precedent. Washington would also, no doubt, have vetoed President Adams's move had he been available for consultation.) Solemn resolutions poured forth from the federal Congress, from the state legislatures, from town meetings up and down the land. Moving eulogies were delivered in London, in Paris, in Amsterdam. Church bells were muffled, mourning rings were worn, black clothing or black sleeve bands were displayed—by some for as long as six months. Eulogists vied with each other to reach, somehow, those oratorical heights that would be worthy of the man— and of the nation. For however great the mourning, the oratory must at the same time explain that the death of George Washington did not mean, would not mean, the death of his nation. Like Franklin, Washington was still present and presiding amongst us.

A memorial service for Washington gathered in that same German Lutheran church in Philadelphia where Washington himself had sat to hear praises poured upon Franklin. Now it was Washington's turn, and the praises were even more effusive, more unrestrained. Congressman Henry Lee, fellow Virginian, rose to pronounce those words known to every schoolchild since: "First in war, first in peace, first in the hearts of his countrymen." Lee observed that "vice shuddered" in Washington's presence, adding that "the purity of his private character gave effulgence to his public virtues." John Adams, correctly perceiving the mood of the country, declared: "For his fellow citizens, if their prayers could have been answered, he would have been immortal." And Jefferson years later, though he offered a somewhat more restrained judgment of Washington's intellect, found no flaw whatsoever in his character: "His integrity was most pure, his justice the most inflexible I have ever known." He was indeed, Jefferson concluded, "in every sense of the words, a wise, a good and a great man." While all strained to do justice to him, Abigail Adams struck the cleanest note: "Simple truth," she wrote, "is his best, his greatest eulogy."[30]

Clergymen of every denomination and region joined in. A careful examination of multitudes of these sermons has revealed how widespread and how elevated was their praise. If Washington had been great in what he gave to America, God was even greater for having given Washington to the nation. Politicians compared Washington to Alexander the Great or to Caesar, but clergymen found biblical parallels most appealing: Washington the great king of Israel, Josiah or Hezekiah or David; or Washington the great leader of Israel, Joshua, or the greatest of them all, Moses. Yale's Timothy Dwight chose his text with care as he prepared his eulogy: "And there arose not a prophet since in Israel like unto Moses, whom the Lord knew face to face" (Deuteronomy 30:10–12). The comparisons were neither vague nor fanciful. "Washington, like Moses, was born of simple, but worthy parents; like Moses, he was trained in the wilderness; like Moses, he reluctantly answered God's call to serve the people." And above all else, of course, like Moses he delivered his people from tyranny and slavery, guiding them toward a new and not-yet-manifest destiny.[31]

Garry Wills has called attention to the comparisons of George Washington to Cincinnatus, the farmer of ancient Rome who left his plow to serve his country but relinquished all power once danger had passed to return to his farm once more. This was another obvious appeal of Washington: he held power as though he held it not. He would wield it, to be sure, but he would not cling to it, lust for it, or refuse to let it go. Benjamin West liked to tell the story of a conversation with King George III, who asked during the Revolution what General Washington would do if he won the war. West replied that Washington would no doubt return to his farm; the startled monarch declared, "If he did that, he would be the greatest man in the world." He, of course, not only did that after the Revolution but was quite prepared to retire after one term as president and insisted on doing so after two.[32] Clergymen, along with many of their fellow citizens, also found the Cincinnatus image appealing since many shared a Whig suspicion of power, particularly of power absolute and unchecked. To be able to govern a nation, citizens must first prove their ability to govern themselves. In this, too, Washington was the "polar star."

Like Moses, Washington led; like Moses, he was not a great speaker; like Moses, he won no reputation as a sophisticated theologian. His actions were his most eloquent words and his very presence his most forceful declaration. He wrote no treatise on military strategy, formulated no system of political theory, and composed no creed—not even of Franklin's modest and generalized kind. Washington did talk about religion, but more in national than in private terms. An Anglican vestryman, he was baptized, married, and buried in the church of his childhood. But he wore denominational labels as lightly as theological ones. "In politics as in religion," he wrote in 1795, "my tenets are few and simple."[33] That rare bit of introspection was directly on target.

He did, of course, use the language of faith, but scarcely of any particular, readily identifiable faith. He acknowledged the all-powerful, if often inscrutable, Providence that governs human affairs and the destiny of nations. At the close of the American Revolution, he responded to a compliment by saying that "the praise is due to the *Grand Architect* of the Universe; who did not see fit to suffer his Superstructures and justice to be subjected to the ambition of the princes of the World, or to the rod of oppression, in the hands of any power upon Earth."[34] That phrase, "Grand

Architect," was wholly characteristic of Washington's many allusions to God: they all possessed a vaguely impersonal, broadly benign, calmly rational flavor. The "Governor of the Universe," "Higher Cause," "Great Ruler of Events," "All Wise Creator," "the Supreme Dispenser of all Good"—these and similar expressions constituted Washington's usual mode of religious discourse.[35]

In the framing of the Constitution, as in the winning of the Revolution, George Washington again saw the steady providential hand. "To that superintending Power alone is our retraction from the brink of ruin to be attributed."[36] And when events did not turn out so well—the radicalism of the French Revolution, for example—this represented no diminution in the strength of "that superintending power": it only demonstrated the limits of our own understanding. At times, we must simply acknowledge that the ways of Providence are "beyond the reach of mortal scan." But never can one doubt that direction, purpose, and meaning are all there, fixed into the foundations of the universe, and this remains true despite our inability always to discern this Grand Plan. When Patrick Henry died in 1799—only a few months before Washington's own death, the nation's first president observed that "the ways of Providence are inscrutable, and can not be scanned by short sighted man; whose duty is submission, without repining at its decrees."[37] In classical terms, Washington was far more the Apollonian than the Dionysiac; in religious terms, he was far more the rationalist than the enthusiast. With a faith as aloof as the man who harbored it, Washington rose far above controversy, thereby enhancing even more his potential as icon.

Though the cool deism of Washington can hardly be distinguished in broad outline from that of Jefferson, the public reaction to the two men and their religious views differed sharply. Only Jefferson was denounced as the "howling atheist," never Washington. Only Jefferson was attacked as the enemy of the churches and the clergy, never Washington. A curious public probed and punched Adams, Franklin, and Jefferson for more detail regarding their Christian convictions, but never Washington. His even-handed tolerance of all groups, even of Roman Catholics, occasioned neither alarm nor complaint. When in 1789 some Presbyterian elders protested to Washington that the Constitution lacked any explicit recognition "of the only true God and Jesus Christ, whom he hath sent," the imperturbable new president calmly replied that "the path of true piety is so plain as to require but little political direction."[38] George Washington believed in God; he believed in America; he believed that the former watched over and protected the latter. If that sort of generic faith was good enough for Israel's Moses, it was good enough for America's too.

The nation did not wait for Washington's death to express its deep feeling and enormous regard for the man become demigod. Following the victory at Yorktown in 1781, the name of Washington became at least as hallowed as that of Moses and was more frequently on the tongue. The *Pennsylvania Journal* confessed that "all panegyrick is vain, and language too feeble to express our ideas of his greatness." Hailed as the country's savior, he was feted, dined, courted, cheered all the way from Virginia to Philadelphia. If he was too exhausted to accept any more of the crowd's applause, no matter. Charles Willson Peale thoughtfully decorated his own house with "transparencies" that honored the hero and appeased the multitude. The level of restraint is evident in Ezra Stiles's election sermon, preached in Connecticut in 1783: "O Washington! how do I love thy name! How have I often adored and blessed thy God, for creating and forming thee the great ornament of human kind! . . . our very enemies stop the madness of their fire in full volley . . . as if rebuked from Heaven with a 'Touch not mine Anointed, and do my Hero no harm!' "[39]

Washington had it all to do over again when, inevitably, he was elected president of these loosely United States. His progression from Mount Vernon to Philadelphia, thence to New York, was not royal: it was finer than that. "Triumphal arches were erected, roses strewn in his path by girls dressed in white, and lyrics sung to Handel's 'See the Conquering Hero Come.' "[40] At the actual moment of inauguration, church bells rang out, ship's cannons in New York's harbor fired away, bands played, fire crackers exploded, as Robert Livingston intoned: "Long live George Washington, President of the United States!"[41] As John Adams was later to say, If the prayers of Americans had been answered, George Washington would have been immortal.

Washington's First Inaugural Address did nothing to lessen the religious fervor surrounding and supporting him. When the new president tendered his homage "to the Great Author of every public and private good," he did so with the assurance that he expressed the sentiments of the American people no less than his own. "No People can be bound to acknowledge and adore the invisible hand, which conducts the Affairs of men more than the People of the United States. Every step, by which they have advanced to the character of an independent nation, seems to have been distinguished by some token of providential agency."[42] Those who heard the address, or more likely read it (for Washington's delivery was scarcely audible), would credit that invisible hand for having been so gracious as to allow this Moses to enter the promised land with his people. Not only would he enter, but he would lead for eight critical, precedent-setting years. And when he at last laid down public duties, Washington again turned attention from himself to "the foundation of the fabric": that is, to religion and morality as the "great Pillars of human happiness, [the] firmest props of the duties of Men and citizens."[43]

These words of the Farewell Address notwithstanding, grieving citizens found their pillar and prop initially to be Washington himself. Three weeks after the hero's death, William Woolley executed a painting, an allegorical memorial, that revealed the apotheosis of George Washington to be already well under way (see Figure 4). Engravings or mezzotints of this painting were purchased by an eager public informed by this advertisement: "On the left is Liberty. On the right is Justice. And the centre represents Virtue holding over the Portrait her Crown, and pointing to Heaven as the reward of her Hero." In addition, the painting included female figures representing Poetry, History, and America ("a female Aboriginal, whose grief evinces the deep regret impressed on all the minds of real Americans"). Upon the entire

Figure 4

"George Washington," William Wooley. Courtesy of The Historical Society
of Pennsylvania: Baker Collection

scene, a sacred light fell, signaling heaven's full approbation.[44]

Before the end of the year 1800, David Edwin had published "an elegant Engraving of the apotheosis of Washington," this based on a now lost painting by Rembrandt Peale (see Figure 5). In this representation, Washington was wholly ethereal, resting upon the clouds and being welcomed into heaven by generals who had fallen before him. Cupid, "suspended in the air, attentively admiring Washington, [holds] a wreath of immortality over his head." The engraving is entitled *Apotheosis of Washington,* in case—however unlikely—anyone should miss the point. In dogmatic language that all the founding fathers would have rejected, it might even have been called *The Bodily Assumption of the Blessed Hero George.* [45]

About the same time that Edwin's work was being advertised for sale, J. J. Barralet's even more ambitious engraving was in preparation—though not actually released until 1802 (see Figure 6). Here the heavenly translation of Washington combined the symbolism of Greek mythology, Christian iconography, American history, and military bravery. The total impact won for the engraving a wide and appreciative audience. Republished and reengraved many times, this portrayal "was also copied on American canvases, English transfer-printed creamware, and Chinese reverse paintings on glass."[46] Showing the influence of Raphael's *Vision of Ezekiel,* the Barralet engraving made "an overtly religious statement."[47] Classical virtues here joined with the Christian virtues of faith, hope, and charity to raise a leader, an American Moses, to sainthood. To this icon one responded with veneration. America now had a saint to intercede on its behalf, a guardian to watch over a dispirited and bewildered people. This Moses would lead his people from despair to promise, from grief to joy, from uncertainty to victory. No Red Sea or, for that matter, no Mississippi River or Pacific Ocean would daunt America in its flight from tyranny to freedom, from weakness to strength. No pursuing chariots or, for that matter, no English battleships or French schemes would thwart this nation in its rise to glory. There has been no prophet in all Israel like unto this one.

Figure 5

"Apotheosis of Washington," David Edwin (after R. Peale). Courtesy of
National Portrait Gallery, Smithsonian Institution

Figure 6

"Apotheosis of George Washington," John James Barralet. Courtesy of
Metropolitan Museum of Art: William H. Huntington

Pilgrimages to Mount Vernon keep alive Washington's status as icon, even as they testify to his enduring "firstness" in the hearts of his countrymen and women. Mount Vernon is his shrine, and an altogether worthy one. Franklin does not come off quite as well so far as the grandeur of his site is concerned. A city boy, Franklin has been nearly swallowed up by urban development. Urban redevelopment, however, now restores something of the old neighborhood. Yet Franklin's real shrine is the American Philosophical Society Hall, with its portraits, scientific equipment, evidence of organizational genius, and other manifestations of a creative culture that Franklin did so much to stimulate and personify.

In 1790 and again in 1799 the new nation suffered as its mighty men of God proved to be, after all, mere mortals. The ways of Providence were, as Washington observed, indeed inscrutable. That such men should die when their country still had need of them seemed neither just nor right. But that such men had lived! Ah, there was reason for rejoicing and for seeing once more the careful design of the Grand Architect. Whether or not they believed in the Bible was not as important as their replication of it. In gazing upon or kneeling before icons such as these, fellow citizens found their thoughts directed toward that overarching Providence who was beyond them and yet at the same time somehow dwelling among them. A later century might celebrate pluralism and diversity, but what this first generation of Americans required was assurance and unity. Franklin and Washington would not remain icons forever; indeed, today one views their canonization with some ill ease that trust was ever so total, emotion ever so full, rhetoric ever so ornate, and the artist's brush ever so softly sentimental. In the dark and treacherous passage from colonial submission to national assertion, however, what Americans most needed was a strong and steady illumination. In and for their own time Franklin and Washington cast just such a bright and certain light.

5. The *Philosophes:* Adams and Jefferson

In our jaded and cynical day, it is difficult to recapture the sense of excitement, the bubbling optimism, the vision and courage and curiosity that characterized the nation's leadership in its earliest years. Outlandish as it strikes our ears, eighteenth-century revolutionaries really did believe and really did assert that they had it in their power to start the world over again. This is part of what is meant by the Enlightenment and part of the task assumed by those persons called *philosophes.*

Philosophes were not technical philosophers; indeed, they most likely disdained the professional philosophers lost in their own rarefied systems and metaphysical abstractions. If one thinks of the cagey old Franklin, wearing his beaver hat in Paris and enjoying the hospitality of the ladies in their fashionable salons, discoursing with insight and wit on any subject introduced for discussion—if that mental picture is conjured up, one brings the proper connotations to the term *philosophe.* These gentlemen regarded nothing as too sacred to be touched or investigated, nothing as too ancient and respected to be challenged or even overthrown. Their curiosity knew no limits and their intellectual daring no restraint. "I have never," John Adams wrote in 1823, "been afraid of a book."[1] Even multivolume sets daunted him not at all, as he whipped through three volumes of this, a dozen volumes of that, the collected works of the Bollandists in fifty volumes or more. Adams was indeed not afraid of a book—nor of language, art, education, travel, nature, history, even theology. "Let every sluice of knowledge be opened," he wrote as a young man, and from this commitment he rarely backed away despite repeated disillusionments and severe disappointments.[2]

The term *Enlightenment* is harder to define because it is so broad a movement, with differing manifestations in France and England, in Scotland and America. Any description of the Enlightenment must, however, confront two words that are themselves both intricate and diffuse: *Reason* and *Nature*. Both are capitalized because eighteenth-century writers preferred it that way and because the capitalization correctly denotes a personification if not deification of these nouns. The Enlightenment did stand for reason, but only of a certain sort. And the age probably deserved the name of Reason, even though Adams, in exasperation, thundered in 1805:

I am willing you should call this the Age of Frivolity . . . and would not object if you had named it the age of Folly, Vice, Frenzy, Fury, Brutality, Daemons, Buonaparte, Tom Paine, the Age of the Burning Brand and Bottomless Pit: or anything but the Age of Reason.[3]

Nevertheless, all of the *philosophes,* Adams included, had much to say in honor of reason, but surely not any and all kinds of reason. The abstractions of Plato, for example, were dismissed with scorn. Both Adams and Jefferson agreed that little of worth could be found there, Adams going so far as to say he had learned only two things from reading Plato: first, that Franklin found in Plato the idea of excusing farmers and sailors from military service; and, second, that sneezing was a good cure for hiccups. "Accordingly," Adams noted, "I have cured myself and all my Friends of that provoking disorder, for thirty Years with a Pinch of Snuff."[4] Abstract, *a priori* speculation had cost humankind much: it had led to absurdities without number and official "truths" without benefit. The classics were not discarded, of course, but Enlightenment thinkers leaned more to the practical Romans than to the theoretical Greeks, more to Epicureans and Stoics than to Platonists and Neoplatonists. Not all philosophers were disdained, to be sure, but to be admitted to the inner circle, philosophers must pay great attention to experience—like John Locke—or give great weight to common sense—like the thinkers of the Scottish Enlightenment.

In discarding all *a priori* authorities, the *philosophes* attacked biblical revelation over and over. Such so-called revelation did not free people's minds, it shackled them; it brought not peace to the world, but a sword. Revelation did not create knowledge, but blocked every path to learning and every free investigation. In the age of Enlightenment, "Reason" always meant, at the very least, a rejection of revelation. That rejection was necessary so that experience (the only lamp by which my feet are guided, said Patrick Henry) could freely inform, so that common sense (in the understanding of both Thomas Paine and Thomas Reid) could be followed, so that self-evidence (made sacred by Jefferson) could be invoked. The entire scientific revolution of previous centuries must be wholly assimilated and harnessed to help create that world anew. That some doctrine was ancient, traditional, and widely held now became an argument *against* its probable truth, rather than the contrary.

The other much-honored and much-invoked word of the age, *Nature,* could, like Reason, take many shapes. It could mean that which was primitive and original, that which existed before the corrupting influences of civilization and metaphysics distorted the pure simplicity of yore. "Nature" could mean that which was universal, found in all women and men everywhere, regardless of custom and culture and conditioning: that which was natural was that found everywhere, Orient and Occident, Aryan and African, Old World and New. Or, with no great concern about the obvious contradiction, "Nature" could mean not that which existed everywhere, but that which existed nowhere yet ought to exist. The natural was the desirable, the norm to be sought rather than the universality to be described. Any word so rich with meaning, so laden with ambiguity, could find many uses. Thomas Paine, for example, pointed out that in the world of nature never was it the case that the larger body was satellite to the smaller: the moon revolved around the earth, not the reverse. Therefore (and in the world of Enlightenment thought the "therefore" was compelling), how unnatural for a whole continent, America, to revolve around and be dependent upon that small island called England. But in religion, even more than in politics, Nature was teacher, guide, model, and the proper object of adoration. So Adams and Jefferson plunged into that rational and natural world, a world of optimism and challenge, of matchless wonder and endless possibility.

In his youth John Adams (1735–1826) thought to become a minister, but soon realized that his independent opinions would create much difficulty. At the age of twenty-one, therefore, he resolved to become a lawyer, noting that in following law rather than divinity, "I shall have liberty to think for myself without molesting others or being molested myself."[5] His purely personal decision also reflects, however, a societal shift from the clerical profession to the legal profession, this shift reducing ministerial dominance in the revolutionary generation. Nonetheless, Adams's vocational redirection did not turn him away from preoccupation with religion. Born in the midst of theological and ecclesiastical controversy, he began reading books in religion at the age of twelve—and he never stopped.[6] In a letter to his son written in 1816, Adams observed: "For fifty years I have neglected all Sciences but Government and Religion." Now, he admitted, he has given up government, but "the latter still occupies my thoughts."[7] John Adams is not, therefore, here being twisted to serve some special purpose. For Adams, religion was no casual interest, no whimsy of the moment.

Adams's attitudes toward both the Enlightenment and Christianity reveal an ambivalence that helps account for his lifelong wrestling with the subject of religion. Adams praised many features of the Enlightenment, but as his comment about the Age of Reason demonstrated, he was far from uncritical of all that went on under its name. What the Enlightenment had done to release humankind from all intellectual bondage won his highest acclaim: "Let the human mind loose. It must be loose. It will be loose. Superstition and Dogmatism cannot confine it."[8] Elsewhere Adams asserted the "divine right and the sacred duty of private individual judgment." Human authority was only that; it must never impede the investigative right of every individual to seek truth, to discover truth, to proclaim truth.[9] Yet, what of Thomas

Paine who was for so many the truest voice of the age, if not its very embodiment? Adams wasted few words on the "blackguard Paine":[10] "He understood neither government nor religion. From a malignant heart he wrote virulent declamations, which [in] the enthusiastic fury of the times intimidated all men, even Mr. [Edmund] Burke, from answering as he ought. His deism . . . has promoted rather than retarded the cause of revelation. . . . His billingsgate, stolen from [others], will never discredit Christianity."[11] For Adams, Paine's *Age of Reason* did not epitomize the Enlightenment; it betrayed it.

Concerning other Enlightenment figures, Adams was more restrained. Joseph Priestley, who wielded so great an influence over Thomas Jefferson, as we shall see, impressed Adams far less. Priestley had some wit and learning, but Charles Dupuis's writing on the origin of all cults displayed "ten times more learning than Priestley ever possessed."[12] Voltaire came off better, for he helped bring about religious liberty: "he caused as great a Revolution in religion as [Francis] Bacon did in science."[13] Even more extravagantly, Adams referred to Voltaire as "a Napoleon in literature," adding that "no man ever lived who had so much wit as Voltaire."[14] Despite such ardent words, however, Adams also declared: "I believe in Voltaire, as much as in Priestley, that is to say in neither." He would learn from both, but would then pursue a faith "deliberately fixed of my own." As Edith Hamilton long ago observed in *The Greek Way,* one did not become like the Greeks by imitating them, for the Greeks were not imitators. One did not become a *philosophe* through imitation, for Enlightenment thinkers created, not copied—or so was their earnest attempt.

John Adams had good words for Christianity, though to the despair of many he never stopped with just the good words. "The Christian Religion as I understand it is the best," he wrote in 1818.[15] But how did he understand it? Quite simply as a vehicle for bringing to the vast multitudes "the great Principle of the Law of Nature and Nations, Love your Neighbour as yourself, and do to others as you would that others should do to you."[16] But all of

the attention to, and persecution in behalf of, the Athanasian*
subtleties deserves to be obliterated from the face of the earth. In
a sharp letter to the Congregationalist Jedidiah Morse, Adams in
1815 made clear that Morse could teach him nothing about orthodoxy that he did not already know, and know too well; moreover, he believed that Morse's continued "exertions" on behalf of
Trinitarian orthodoxy would "promote the Church philosophic
more than the Church Athanasian, or Presbyterian."[17] And to his
son a few months later, Adams expressed amazement that, after
all that had been written by Samuel Clarke, Daniel Waterland, and
Joseph Priestley, John Quincy persisted in holding to the Athanasian creed.[18] The early fathers—before Athanasius—were much
more liberal than we are today, the father commented, with our
learned and uncharitable doctors "popistical or Presbyterian." It
was simply not the case, and never would be, that only Calvinists
went to heaven![19] Everybody wanted a monopoly on immortality,
Adams complained; each church believes that it alone has the
"Holy Ghost in a Phial, in the bill of a Dove." Rather than permit
this intolerant exclusivism, Adams preferred more honesty and
less hypocrisy: let us "neither betray nor insult each other's Rhap-
sodies."[20]

Men and women should grow in their religious understanding,
Adams advised his daughter-in-law, so that they never fear to
embrace "the truth when we see evidence for it, although it may
contradict our early opinions." Creeds cannot compare with conduct in significance, and the hundred volumes that have been
produced in the Unitarian-Trinitarian controversy will not, cannot
settle the doctrinal dispute. Adams advised anyone troubled about
religious controversy to follow this recipe. Begin with these questions, he wrote: "First. Is this stupendous & immeasureable universe governed by eternal fate? 2. Is it governed by chance? 3. Is
it governed by caprice, anger, resentment & vengeance? 4. Is it
governed by intelligence, wisdom, and benevolence?" The first

---

*Athanasius, church father of the fourth century, was identified with the formal
defining of the doctrine of the Trinity. As such, both Adams and Jefferson scorned
him.

three questions, Adams reported, he had after careful examination decided "forever in the negative." The fourth, on the other hand, had been decided unequivocally in the affirmative, "& from this last decision I have derived all my system of divinity & the first philosophy and have received more joy & comfort in believing it" than in affirming or doubting any of the others.[21] Clearly subjecting himself to something like Descartes's methodological doubt, Adams here found his firm foundation, his unshakable rock in religion.

Despite all doubts, John Adams could now build on that foundation a structure that allowed for at least three major religious assertions: God's almighty power, religion's tie to morality, the necessity of immortality. First, Adams, despite the many angry shots aimed at Calvinism, proclaimed and acclaimed the absolute sovereignty of God. Adams a Calvinist yet! From early entries in his diary to letters written late in life, Adams composed variations on a single theme: God is so great, I am so small. Adams never doubted who was in charge of the universe, never viewed himself as master of his, or anyone's, destiny. Like the Puritan poet Edward Taylor, Adams could ask: "Lord, Can a Crumb of Dust the Earth outweigh,/ Outmatch all mountains, nay the Chrystall Sky?" Adams's questions went like this: "Have I hardiness enough to contend with omnipotence? Or have I cunning enough to elude infinite Wisdom, or ingratitude enough to Spurn at infinite Goodness?"[22]

As a young man, these were his questions; as an old man, these were his assurances: "I say that if I had not steadfastly believed in a Government of the Universe, wise beyond my comprehension, and benevolent beyond my conception, I should have been constantly not only in dejection but in despair, for at least 55 years of my life."[23] A faithful reader of Isaac Newton (as of nearly everyone else), Adams thought that Newton's resolving all natural force "into the agency of the supreme being" was "as philosophical as it was pious." Needing no particular help from Newton, however, Adams had already approached the universe with reverence and awe: "I veil my face like a Seraph and cry holy! holy!

holy! Worm! confine thyself to thy dust. Do thy duty in thy own sphere."[24] Whenever Adams spent any time thinking about the stars, the Milky Way, the "Stupendous orbits of Suns," planets and satellites and comets, "I feel an irresistible impulse to fall on my knees in Adoration of the Power that moves, the Wisdom that directs, and the Benevolence that Sanctifies this wonderful whole."[25] In much of this Adams revealed what can only be called a kind of Edwardian joy in ascribing sovereignty above all others to God, with its concomitant humbling of his wormlike self. Also, Adams displayed a stoic resignation to the Cosmic Will, not whining or complaining, but supporting and rejoicing. This is what religion was all about: resignation to God and goodness to humanity.[26]

Second, Adams affirmed and reaffirmed the essential link between religion and morality. Not only were these two necessarily joined, but only in keeping the two together could the new nation survive. In a famous letter to his cousin and Congregational minister, Zabdiel Adams, the political Adams—in the midst of the Revolutionary struggle—wrote:

Statesmen, my dear Sir, may plan and speculate for liberty, but it is religion and morality alone which can establish the principles upon which freedom can securely stand. The only foundation of a free constitution is pure virtue.

Without virtue, people may change governments but in so doing they only trade one tyranny for another. Adams encouraged his clerical cousin to pull "down the strong-holds of Satan." Then, realizing all this might sound a little too pat, a bit too forced, Adams added: "This is not cant, but the real sentiment of my heart."[27] The doctrine of Original Sin had no appeal for Adams, because it allowed a cheap and easy escape from moral responsibility. "I am answerable for my own sins," he wrote in 1815, because "I know they were my own faults; and that is enough for me to know."[28] Don't speak to me of vicarious merit and vicarious punishment: these "are contradictions in terms. Guilt is consciousness of fault. A steals a Diamond: how can *B* be conscious of the crime?"[29]

And what in this new age can now be said regarding that centuries-old quarrel about free will and liberty? Adams replied: "If there is no liberty, there is no responsibility. No Virtue, No Vice, No Merit or Demerit, No Reward and no Punishment." Adams asserted himself to be free and accountable, "how poor soever my Account may be."[30] Unlike Jefferson, Adams found materialism a thoroughly objectionable doctrine, because it made everything mechanical and fixed, without life or power or "motion, action, thought, sensation, reflection, reason, and Sentiment." A universe of that character Adams neither believed in nor cared to affirm. To the Newtons, Diderots, and d'Holbachs, Adams spoke: "Ye know nothing of causes, and little of effects. Ye know enough of your duties: attend to them. Be good fathers, sons, brothers, neighbors, friends, patriots, and philanthropists, good subjects and Citizens of the Universe, and trust the ruler with his skies."[31] Know your duty, then do it. This is what all proper religion taught and is what all proper religion helped human beings to perform. Indeed, Adams confessed to Benjamin Rush, without religion the Adamses "would have been rakes, fops, sots, gamblers, starved with hunger, frozen with cold, scalped by Indians &c., &c., &c."[32]

So much emphasis did Adams place on morality that he stood in grave danger of being accused of orthodoxy! He tried repeatedly to make it clear that, though a "church-going animal," he was not guilty of trying to foist off an establishment of Presbyterianism upon the country. And though, when president, he went so far as to proclaim national fasts in 1798 and 1799, he was not trying to rewrite the Constitution, either of the nation or of Massachusetts. Convinced that his recommending of fasts had "turned him out of office," he explained to Rush that his enemies charged that his declaration had somehow come straight from the General Assembly of the Presbyterian church. On the contrary, Adams protested, "I had no concern" or connection with that.

That Assembly has alarmed and alienated Quakers, Anabaptists, Mennonites, Moravians, Swedenborgians, Methodists, Catholics, Protestant Episcopalians, Arians, Socinians, Arminians, &c. A general suspicion prevailed that the Presbyterian Church was ambitious and aimed at an establishment of a national church. I was represented as a Presbyterian and at the head of this political and ecclesiastical project. The secret whisper ran through all the sects, "Let us have Jefferson, Madison, Burr, anybody . . . rather than a Presbyterian President."[33]

Adams stood for morality, but he also stood for liberty, and that has never been an easy distinction to maintain, whether in the eighteenth century or the twentieth.

Third, John Adams affirmed immortality, finding in this doctrine an ingredient essential to a moral system of governance. "A future state will set all right; without the supposition of a future state I can make nothing of this Universe, but a Chaos."[34] Indeed, "if I did not believe in a future State, I should believe in no God." The universe in such a case would, even "with all its swelling Pomp," be only "a boyish Fire Work."[35] Of course, Adams did not believe that a trip to heaven should be treated as some kind of cosmic lottery or that hope for a blissful eternity should be nothing more than yet another manifestation of self-interest. In every religion, some paradise is held out as the lure, with the strong suggestion that only persons of this or that sect will ever find eternal happiness. Adams did not ever expect wholly to eradicate self-love and narrow parochialism, but he did "wish that all had a little more Charity for those who differ from them."[36]

Deists, it is often said, believe in God, freedom, and immortality. This description fits John Adams without difficulty, but freedom was present chiefly as the necessary condition for morality. Belief in God, morality, and immortality might be an even better "creed" for Adams, though creeds had so little appeal for him that it is no doubt wiser to impose none upon him. (As John Adams wrote to his daughter-in-law in 1821: "I do not however attach much importance to creeds because I believe he cannot be wrong whose life is right.") To appreciate more fully what Adams did believe, however, it is necessary also to examine what he chose to reject.

First, like Jefferson, Adams denounced the priestcraft and corrupted revelation that had changed a pure gospel of Jesus into a crafty combination of superstition, knavery, and hypocrisy. I know of no divine authority, Adams wrote, for Lords Popes or Lords Cardinals or Lords Bishops, but neither do I know of any divine authority for "Lords Parsons, Lords Brethren, Lords Councils, Lords Synods, Lords Associations, Lords Consociations, or Lords General Assemblies." All that any of these "Lords" have been good for is "to deliver a man over to Satan to be buffeted."[37] The clergy in our own time, Adams observed, behave too much like clergy of other lands and other days: "making themselves the willing instruments of an ignorant popularity [or] an insolent Oligarchy." He had "heard some of the grossest newspaper slanders trumpetted from the pulpit against the most important men in the nation," and of course Adams was himself among those trumpeted against.[38] For the sake of both liberty and religion, we must rid ourselves of all "sacerdotal despotism."[39] Jesuits constituted Adams's favorite example of such despotism, but clergy closer to home did not escape his sharp rebuke. In Newburyport, he had been told, nine clergymen dwelled who could not be civil to one another. They would not invite each other to their pulpits, nor could any one of them gain the pulpit of another church. Now, Adams reported, a person asked to subscribe to a missionary society declined, but countered with this offer: "If you will raise a fund to send Missionaries to Newburyport to Convert these Nine Clergymen to Christianity, I will contribute as much as any Man."[40]

Second, Bible societies and missionary societies aroused the ire of Braintree's *philosophe.* If the clergy insist on sending Bibles and evangelists all over the world, Adams argued that equity required that the translations of the sacred books of all the world's religions be sent to America. The Crusades were invented to keep the barons from destroying the powers of kings and popes, Adams wrote, and "these Bible Societies have been invented by deeper Politicians still to divert mankind from the study and pursuit of their Natural Rights. I wish Societies were formed in India, China, & Turkey to send us gratis translations of their Sacred Books; one good turn deserves another."[41] If people look for truth in the faith of others, Adams argued, some truth can usually be found. In any case, he confessed, he could not work up his mind to such a pitch as to believe "that all these millions and millions of men are to be miserable and only a handful of Elect Calvinists happy forever."[42] Though it would be as good for us to receive missionaries as to send them, does anyone really think our "reverend gentlemen w[oul]d be tolerant enough to permit them?" More than likely, they would "try to inflame the civil power to raise its arm of flesh and strength to drive them out."[43] John Adams, too much a product of the Enlightenment, too much the *philosophe,* refused to cram this person's dogma down that one's throat: "Let the mind loose."

Third, Adams entertained grave suspicion of religious revivalism, awakenings, and enthusiasm. Having grown up in the waning days of New England's first Awakening, he had had his heart and his mind filled to overflowing with the religious acrimony of the time. By the time of his maturity he had learned to look askance at all passionate upheavals in religion. True, Christianity "is the religion of the heart: but the heart is deceitful above all things, and unless controuled by the dominion of the head, will lead us into Salt Ponds." Whether "Awakenings" were political or religious, Adams questioned them. We swing like pendulums from one extreme to another, Adams observed, for "mankind must have a crusade, a war of reformation, a French Revolution, or Anti-Revolution to amuse them and preserve them from Ennui."[44] The revivalist, George Whitefield, he described as "that great model of theatrical grace & Elegance of harmonious Oratory and att the same time . . . of fervent piety."[45] Many persons, recalling that first Great Awakening, now wished for a national revival, being persuaded (to Adams's dismay) that there must be only one religion in the country and, indeed, the world. John Wesley, Adams characterized as "one of the most remarkable Characters that enthusiasm, superstition, fanaticism ever produced." Nothing in imagination can be as whimsically extravagant as this enthusiasm called Methodism.[46] And even William Penn, who had "a great and powerful mind," could as theologian be compared only with Wesley or Zinzendorf or Swedenborg, and all these taken together would not amount to one Montesquieu.[47] Human beings were born not only to be free but to be rational as well; yet, they let the heart rule the head and the impetuosity of the moment sweep everything before it. Anxiously Adams inquired: Will mankind be credulous dupes forever?[48]

In the second decade of the nineteenth century, Adams felt that the world and its ways were leaving him far behind; everything appeared to flow around him, no longer through him. Way off in Braintree in retirement and isolation, far from power, far from the whirl of the world, he had become an anachronism. But happily Philadelphia's Benjamin Rush managed in 1812 to bring Jefferson and Adams together, these former patriotic allies and one-time good friends. Now years of political enmity divided them: each had leveled charges against the other; each felt abused and misused by the other. As long as Jefferson was in office, no reconciliation was possible. Four years out of the presidency, Jefferson in Monticello, also far from the world's whirl, might find the revival of an old friendship as welcome as would the Braintree recluse. Adams took the first tentative step early in 1812, sending Jefferson some published writings of his son, John Quincy. Jefferson replied warmly, and within a year, the most remarkable correspondence between former presidents that this nation has ever seen sprang into full flower.

Of course, Jefferson too was a man of the Enlightenment, a *philosophe* who would not only fight against all that hobbled human minds but would exercise the hard-won intellectual freedom to probe and query, to speculate and compose, to reflect and refine. Even more than Adams, Jefferson gave sustained and systematic attention to affirmations about religion. It was one thing to rail against priestcraft and ecclesiastical tyranny, to denounce superstition and dogmatism; it was quite another to assert more positively what a rational person living in an enlightened age might believe, might affirm, might stand for. Through the instrumentality of the leading English divine Richard Price, Jefferson learned of books that would help him answer some of his own religious questions, particularly those concerning the doctrine of the Trinity. Through Price, Jefferson was introduced not only to new books, but more crucially to the chemist and theologian and Unitarian Joseph Priestley.

In 1793 Priestley published a lengthy work entitled *An History of the Corruptions of Christianity,* an exposé of what early Christian theologians had done to mystify, Hellenize, Platonize, and generally corrupt the pure primitive gospel of Jesus Christ. When Jefferson read and reread this work in the 1790s, he saw new doors of understanding open wide before him. He thought that he had rejected Christianity; now he realized that it was only the corruptions of Christianity that he had rejected! Those corruptions, unfortunately, so pervaded all of Christendom that the genuine article was lost almost beyond rescue. But Christianity must be rescued! For many other persons would repeat this same mistake, concluding that Christianity was just what all the priests and Platonists declared it to be. What a tragedy it would be, Jefferson recognized, should such a mistake prevent them from ever embracing the simple command, "Fear god and love thy neighbor." Here, underneath all the priestly absurdity and accretion lay a pure gospel, a gospel ready to be delivered out of the hands of the necromancers and soothsayers into the hands of all enlightened humanity.

Instead of abandoning Christianity, Jefferson was about to discover Christianity. Rather than the infidel, the atheist, the enemy of all religion and the destroyer of all social order, Jefferson might become another mighty reformer, the harbinger of yet another Reformation. "It is only by Banishing Hierophantic mysteries and Scholastic subtleties . . . and getting back to the plain and unsophisticated precepts of Christ," he wrote, "that we become *real* Christians." And why should such a task have eluded so many for so long? Because, Jefferson replied, the priests have conspired to keep the gospel obscure and abstract. The pure and primitive gospel "gives no scope to make dupes; priests could not live by it."[49]

In 1803, while riding back to Washington from Monticello, President Thomas Jefferson read another small book of Priestley's: *Socrates and Jesus Compared.* This writing of Priestley's was better yet, for it came from a scholar who really knew the classics (as Jefferson did), was prepared to acknowledge their merits, but could go beyond them to show why the message of Jesus was still essential to humankind. Jefferson could hardly wait to reach the White House, where, in his excitement and thrill, he wrote Priestley of "the pleasure I had in the perusal" of this booklet and of "the desire it excited to see you take up the subject on a more extensive scale."[50] Such intellectual stimulation moved Jefferson to state more explicitly than before something of his own conclusions about religion. He offered to Priestley this swift outline that he hoped, someday, to have time to fill in more completely.

I would begin, he said, with the ancients, doing "justice to the branches of morality they have treated well"; then, to the Jews, showing in what respects they needed a reformation; then, to the "master workman," Jesus, demonstrating "that his system of morality was the most benevolent and sublime probably that has been ever taught; and eminently more perfect than those of any of the ancient philosophers." Jefferson could only regret that this sublime system has over eighteen centuries been so "disfigured and sophisticated" that many rational persons "throw off the whole system in disgust."[51] But this is only my outline, Jefferson informed Priestley; he needed more time and more information to do justice to it. For the moment, he had time only to reflect.

When Jefferson reflected, however, he usually wrote. Ten days after this letter to Priestley, Jefferson wrote to a Massachusetts shipmaster explaining why the ancients needed the complementary teachings of Jesus. The moral philosophers of Greece and Rome were concerned chiefly with "the government of our passions . . . and the procuring our own tranquility. On our duties to others they were short and deficient." Jesus, on the other hand, embraced "with charity and philanthropy, our neighbors, our countrymen, and the whole family of mankind." Earlier thinkers, moreover, confined their attention to external deeds, while Jesus did not stop there: "he pressed his scrutinies into the region of our thoughts, and called for purity at the fountain head."[52]

Then just two days later, Jefferson addressed a letter to that faithful Philadelphia friend Benjamin Rush. Many years earlier Jefferson had promised to give Rush a fuller statement of his own religious faith. But in the early 1790s he was not ready to do so. Now, in the early 1800s, he was more nearly ready to tell Rush, privately, what he believed. He wanted his religious views to remain private because once one started talking about one's religion openly the public quickly concluded that it had a right to know—everything! If public opinion ever became itself a kind of Inquisition, then the First Amendment lost all force and effect. "It behooves every man," Jefferson wrote, "who values liberty of conscience for himself, to resist invasions of it in the case of others." But with that cautious proviso, Jefferson now unveiled his inner thoughts to his trusted friend.

I am not anti-Christian, Jefferson explained, only anticorruption. With respect to the "genuine precepts of Jesus himself," "I am a real Christian . . . sincerely attached to his doctrines, in preference to all others." To illustrate what this assertion meant, Jefferson filled in some of that sketchy outline provided to Priestley just a few weeks earlier. He repeated his concern about the moral teachings of the Greeks: namely, that they centered only on self, ignoring all responsibility to others. But then, Jefferson conceded, we must allow for the fact that the Greeks may have suffered, just as Jesus had, at the hands of their disciples and priests. Their purest teachings may simply not have survived.

The ancient Jews were deists, Jefferson noted, but the attributes associated with their deity "were degrading and injurious." Their ethics, moreover, "were not only imperfect, but often irreconcileable with the sound dictates of reason." So the ethics of the classical world were defective, as were those of the Hebraic world. Jesus was needed, and Jesus appeared: a man of obscure parentage, poor circumstances, and no education. Fortunately, however, his natural endowments were great and his eloquence sublime. His fate, however, like that of Socrates, was to leave us nothing directly from his own pen. In the case of Jesus, his sublime teachings fell into the hands of "the most unlettered, and ignorant of men." Thus, his teachings have reached us in a form that is "mutilated, misstated, and often unintelligible."

This tragedy is compounded by his "schismatising followers" who have engrafted upon what pure pearls he did leave behind "the mysticisms of a Graecian Sophist, frittering them into subtleties, and obscuring them with jargon." I do not debate or discuss the matter of inspiration, said Jefferson; I am concerned solely with "the intrinsic merit of his doctrines." And what did Jesus in his pure, unbarnacled teaching do? He returned us to the Jewish idea of one God, away from all the polytheism of Greece and Rome, but he gave us "juster notions of his attributes and government." Moreover, he corrected the defective ethics of antiquity by "gathering all into one family, under the bonds of love, charity, peace, common wants, and common aids." Finally, he taught us "emphatically, the doctrine of a future state."[53]

Here, in brief compass, Jefferson offered his "Syllabus": his own view of history, morality, divinity, and erroneous philosophy. He sent copies to a few friends, including Priestley and later John Adams. But he warned all to keep this Syllabus to themselves, for the clergy would love to get their hands on it in order to make me "the butt of every set of disquisitions which every priest would undertake to write on every tenet it expresses." Worse than that, it might provoke another whole plague of theological controversy, "repeating in new forms all the volumes of divinity which are now mouldering on the shelves from which they should never more be taken."[54] When one correspondent in reply urged Jefferson to write a whole book on religion, the latter rejoined in horror that he would never do such a thing. "I should as soon think of writing for the reformation of Bedlam, as of the world of religious sects. . . . I not only write nothing on religion, but rarely permit myself to speak on it, and never but in a reasonable company."[55] But he did write a book, though he did not think of it as a presentation of his views; rather, it only rescued those pearls long buried, obscured, hidden from view.

If Jefferson's religion rested upon the "genuine precepts" of Jesus, then somehow one must salvage those precepts, must separate the wheat from the chaff, must dig the diamonds out of all that dung. Joseph Priestley seemed the ideal man to do just that. Early in 1804 Jefferson wrote to urge Priestley to prepare a digest of the moral teachings of Jesus, leaving out all that had been added later or was obviously extraneous to the simple gospel. Such a compendium, Jefferson observed, "would be short and precious." Meanwhile, Jefferson would work with Bibles in Greek and English, picking out those "morsels of morality" that constituted Jesus' great contribution to the world. Priestly, however, did not live to complete the task that Jefferson pressed upon him, dying that same year. The burden of distilling the teachings of Jesus fell, therefore, to Jefferson. He had time in 1804 only for an English version of the "Philosophy of Jesus," no copy of which survives.[56] But a decade or so after leaving the White House, Jefferson completed the more ambitious *Life and Morals of Jesus,* plumbing the Greek, Latin, French, and English versions of the New Testament available to him for those words superbly crafted by the world's master workman.

No biblical scholar, no trained exegete, no expert in ancient manuscripts or textual traditions, Jefferson would determine that which was genuine by the "style and spirit" of the words. In that earlier, now lost work, Jefferson had had no difficulty in separating the genuine from the false, he stated, though he had done it all too hastily. It was "the work of one or two evenings only, while I lived at Washington, overwhelmed with other business: and it is my intention to go over it again at more leisure."[57] In his more deliberate work, accomplished in retirement at Monticello, Jefferson still found "the work obvious and easy," as one could readily separate keen insight from palpable charlatanism, correct morality from "so much absurdity." The former president concluded that the apostle Paul was the first corrupter, he being to Jesus as Plato was to Socrates. Jefferson therefore winnowed, and with what result?

He included the birth of Jesus (following Luke), but omitted all angels and heavenly pronouncements regarding the event. Proceeding to the baptism of Jesus and the latter's calling of his disciples, Jefferson hurried on to his major interest: the Sermon on the Mount. Long teaching sections chosen from both Matthew and Luke emphasized obedience to the spirit rather than the law. Jefferson ignored all claims by Jesus to being divine and exhibited no interest in the extended discussion of "Who is the Christ?" When Jesus performed a miracle in connection with some teaching, the teaching survived, the miracle did not. Teachings that were apocalyptic in nature (e.g., Mark 13) held no appeal whatever for Jefferson, who found the entire Book of Revelation "merely the ravings of a Maniac"; any commentary beyond that was superfluous, for "what has no meaning admits no explanation."[58] Finally, Jefferson included verses detailing the death of Jesus but not the resurrection. No Easter morning sun rises in Jefferson's "Bible," the last sentence reading: "There laid they Jesus, and rolled a great stone to the door of the sepulchre, and departed."[59] Immortality as a general principle was credible; personal, bodily resurrection was not.

What Jefferson hoped to reveal in this reconstruction of Jesus' life and teaching was a natural, reasonable Christianity, a religion that ennobled the human race and in no way degraded or deluded it. Jefferson's choice of title, "Life and Morals," emphasized the ethical aspect, for, like Adams, Jefferson regarded the bond between religion and morality to be indissoluble. Drawing upon not only Priestley and Price but also Conyers Middleton and Daniel Waterland, Jefferson would make Christianity acceptable to the Enlightenment and the Enlightenment acceptable to Christians. He more nearly succeeded in the latter task than the former.[60]

Like Adams, Jefferson had no difficulty proclaiming the existence of God. Finding the cosmological argument as fully persuasive as did his English counterparts, Jefferson concluded that the human mind could not help but to perceive "in all this design, cause and effect . . . a fabricator of things from matter and motion." This Creator was also a regulator and preserver, even a "regenerator into new and other forms."[61] We learn of this God, to be sure, by consulting nature, not revelation, for only in the former do we confront directly the skill, the design, the power that convinces us of God's existence. Unlike Adams, however, Jefferson found the force of the cosmological argument present only in materialism and not in spirit-ism. "When once we quit the basis of sensation, all is in the wind." God gave us the senses just as he gave us our minds, and neither would deceive us. Materialism instructs us in reality; immaterialism plunges us "into the fathomless abyss of dreams and phantasms."[62] One need not speculate beyond what was already presented to us—plainly and right before our eyes.

Trusting our senses and our reason, said Jefferson, we know that God is. It is far more difficult, however, to know precisely what God is. Jesus spoke of God as a spirit, but he did not define "spirit"—nor, added Jefferson, do I. "I am therefore of his theology, believing that we have neither words nor ideas adequate to that definition."[63] But one attribute of God we can know without waffling ambiguity or metaphysical musing: God is One, not many; single, not plural; a Unity, not a Trinity. The notion of the Trinity was one of those nonsensical propositions that the rational mind can only dismiss. Like John Adams, Thomas Jefferson attributed this absurdity to the fourth-century theologian Athanasius, "and I should as soon undertake to bring the crazy skulls of Bedlam to sound understanding, as to inculcate reason into that of an Athanasian."[64] The doctrine of the Trinity, a "mere Abracadabra," was only the unhappiest example of what happens when one gave up "morals for mysteries, Jesus for Plato."[65]

Once all this was carefully explained to an enlightened age, "the incomprehensible jargon of Trinitarian arithmetic" must soon be surrendered.[66] All will come to recognize the unity of God, just as Jesus did. "The religion of Jesus is founded on the Unity of God, and this principle, chiefly, gave it triumph over the rabble of heathen gods then acknowledged. Thinking men of all nations rallied readily to the doctrine of one only god."[67] If thinking men managed that even in the first century, certainly they should be able to manage it now in the nineteenth. "I have little doubt," Jefferson wrote in 1822 (just four years before his death), that "the whole of our country will soon be rallied to the Unity of the

Creator." Indeed, the whole world would never have abandoned that standard of One God had not the "religion-builders" so distorted and deformed "the doctrines of Jesus, so muffled them in mysticisms, fancies, and falsehoods. . . . Had there never been a Commentator, there never would have been an infidel."[68] Once primitive Christianity was fully restored, displacing totally "the hocus-pocus phantasm" of Athanasius and company, Christianity would escape all danger of being eclipsed or superseded. "I confidently expect," Jefferson wrote in 1822, "that the present generation will see Unitarianism become the general religion of the United States."[69] And to the Harvard professor and Unitarian Benjamin Waterhouse, Jefferson that same year observed: "I trust that there is not a young man now living in the U. S. who will not die an Unitarian."[70]

Like Adams, who also considered himself a Unitarian for more than sixty years, Jefferson saw the test of religion to reside in its link to morality. "The sum of all religion as expressed by it's best preacher, 'fear god and love thy neighbor,' contains no mystery, needs no explanation."[71] "It is in our lives, and not from our words, that our religion must be read."[72] If I were to found a new sect, Jefferson observed in 1819, my fundamental principle "would be the reverse of Calvin's, that we are saved by our good works which are within our power, and not by our faith which is not within our power."[73] So strongly did Jefferson feel about the necessity of public virtue that he was even willing, should it come to that, to have a perverted and corrupted Christianity rather than none at all. For no system of morality would work for the common man or woman "without the sanction of divine authority stampt upon it."[74] We need not settle for an adulterated version of the Christian religion, however, when a cleansed copy is so nearly within our grasp.

Poor old Athanasius, poor old John Calvin, even poor old Samuel Hopkins—they all suffered terrible blows across the head, along with poor old Plato, whom Jefferson did not find instructive even in the matter of hiccups. Plato, Jefferson wrote to an agreeing John Adams, was filled with whimsies, fancies, and fog. Reading him again, Jefferson found it "the heaviest task-work I ever went through. . . . While wading thro' the whimsies, the puerilities, and unintelligible jargon . . . I laid it down often to ask myself how it could have been that the world should have so long consented to give reputation to such nonsense as this?"[75] And Calvin? He and his followers have "introduced more new absurdities into the Christian religion" than can readily be imagined or than should be tolerated. To all the Platonists and to all the Calvinists, let us declare that "our saviour did not come into the world to save metaphysicians only."[76]

What was all so simple had been made all too subtle. What was freely available "to the simplest understanding" had now become privileged, secretive, esoteric truth to be whispered from behind the altars of the mighty. The Calvinists have not perpetuated Christianity, they have perverted and defeated it. "Their blasphemies have driven thinking men into infidelity," and had it not been for their "Counter-religion," "the whole civilised world would now have been Christian." Only one significant difference can be detected between paganism and Calvinism, Jefferson wrote Jared Sparks in 1820: paganism is far more intelligible.[77] Tongue in cheek, John Adams once wished Jefferson good health and long life until he became a Calvinist. A wish like that, Jefferson replied, if granted, "would make me immortal."[78]

Like Adams, Jefferson asserted the oneness and wonder of God; like Adams, Jefferson joined religion fixedly to morality, and found the moral instinct "to be the brightest gem with which the human character is studded";[79] and, like Adams, Jefferson found immortality to be an attractive idea chiefly because it, too, was fixedly joined to morality. With respect to his own personal immortality, Jefferson spoke with restraint, if not doubt. In this dark realm, reason could not take us very far, so faith had to fill the gap. I am content, Jefferson declared, "to trust for the future to him who has been so good for the past."[80] Our knowledge in this shadowy business, he told Adams in 1820, can never be complete, but Jefferson did not mind being ignorant with respect to his own life after death and its exact nature. In fact, "ignorance, in these cases, is truly the softest pillow on which I can lay my head."[81]

But if unsure with respect to his personal fate, Jefferson emphatically asserted the general truth of immortality. Justice and good must ultimately prevail, else this was not a moral universe. Since in this life virtue was not always rewarded and justice did not always triumph, then the moral instincts of human nature demanded some "future state of rewards and punishments." Moreover, if a moral sense was built into our very nature, as Jefferson asserted it to be, the Creator who implanted this sense in our breasts would surely also implant a moral structure into the cosmos itself. The doctrine of immortality, then, proclaimed the moral nature of God and of the universe that came from his hand. Moreover, Jesus taught "the doctrine of a future state . . . and wielded it with efficacy, as an important incentive, supplementary to the other motives to moral conduct." In fact, one of the clear "improvements" over Judaism was Jesus' addition of a belief in immortality.[82] God, freedom, *and* immortality.

Beginning in 1812, these two old political warriors and now retired statesmen took up their endlessly fascinating correspondence with each other. They softened their earlier political differences, shared their philosophical prejudices, reinforced their religious convictions, and voiced their anxieties concerning their new nation. World events sometimes overwhelmed them as they feared that an age of darkness might succeed the age of light. Slavery confounded them as Jefferson dreaded another Peloponnesian war and Adams regretted that he had "none of the genius of Franklin, to invent a rod to draw from the cloud [of slavery] its Thunder and lightning."[83] And, not unnaturally, they even worried a bit about their own reputations in history. Adams was prepared to let posterity judge which of the two former presidents had been more nearly correct in his administration.[84] But posterity lost interest in nonimportation agreements and embargoes—at least as they related to Adams and Jefferson. On the other hand, posterity could never forget, and would if necessary readily forgive, two men who had the exquisite sense of timing both to die on the Fourth of July, 1826, precisely one half century after the signing of the Declaration of Independence.

One question that posterity does toss around is what to call these men: Christians, deists, rationalists, freethinkers, *philosophes,* Unitarians, radicals, iconoclasts, men of their own time or men ahead of their time. The Christian label was both embraced and rejected by the two themselves. Jefferson declared himself a Christian, "a *real Christian,* that is to say, a disciple of the doctrines of Jesus, very different from the Platonists."[85] But, of course, he denied the divinity of Jesus (and, against Priestley, the divinity even of his mission) and announced on one occasion that "I am of a sect by myself, as far as I know."[86] When rumors circulated that Jefferson had been converted to some brand of orthodoxy, he exploded that these rumors came from the same sources that had branded him "Atheist, Deist; or Devil." Now, these clergymen claim me as a convert in a vain effort to use me as "a boulster for their duperies." But I won't allow it: "My opinion is that there would never have been an infidel, if there had never been a priest."[87]

John Adams could explode too, and the notion of "innumerable millions" being consigned to eternal torment, "miserable forever," set him off. Why would an all-powerful, all-charitable, all-wise God do that or permit such a thing to happen? For his own glory, we are told by the orthodox.

What is his Glory? Is he ambitious? does he want promotion? Is he vain? tickled with Ambition? Exulting and tryumphing in his Power and the Sweetness of his Vengeance? Pardon me, my Maker, for these Aweful Questions. My Answer to them is always ready: I believe no such Things.[88]

But the question remained: Does that make me no Christian? Adams knew what the answer would be from the "Calvinistick" and "Athanasian Divines." "Ye will say, I am no Christian: I say Ye are no Christians: and there the Account is ballanced."[89] And what both Adams and Jefferson would say beyond this was that honest people know that they are groping in the dark and that the universe in all of its majesty and mystery cannot be boxed and compassed by mere insects or worms.

One of the ironies regarding our two *philosophes* is that they say repeatedly that they will not talk about, will not discuss, religion; they then proceed to talk about and discuss very little else. They denounce at length the tyrants in religion, the obscurantists, the "pence and power" seekers. They affirm at length the role of reason, the central place of morality, the Infinity that defines their own finitude and limits their own wisdom. And they both ask that their religion, as well as that of all others, be judged by their lives. Mere words, facile labels, tell us little, whereas long and event-filled lives tell us much. Rejecting the labels, therefore, and examining the lives, one can only conclude that both Adams and Jefferson had within them the essence of the religious spirit. They could without difficulty or hesitation join in the prayer of the Breton fisherman, "O God, thy sea is so great, and my boat is so small. Amen."

6. The Churches and the People

The ratification of the Constitution in 1787 and 1788 did more than establish a new government for the United States; it established a new base of sovereignty: namely, the people rather than the states. "We the people" in special ratification conventions gave approbation to that document drawn up in the long, hot Philadelphia summer of '87, putting the nation into a sharply different mode of operation than that which had prevailed under the Articles of Confederation. Just how much of their own authority the states had yielded was much debated, but that national sovereignty would and must prevail ultimately became clear.

So also in religion as in politics the people moved into a role of greater participation and control. No longer did the churches belong to the colonies or to the states; now they belonged to the people. And those denominations that most readily adjusted to this new circumstance prospered most conspicuously in the opening decades of the nineteenth century. Those who clung to establishments or even to the idea of establishment had greater difficulty breaking out of their traditional boundaries, both ecclesiastical and geographical. But those who preached their gospel directly to the people, openly and freely and unconditionally, found among those people, male and female, black and white, a ready response.

In many respects, conditions in the early nineteenth century did not augur well for institutional religion in America. The firm foundations set down in the colonial era had been rudely shaken by a Revolution that was more anticlerical than most historians recognize, by a Constitution that acknowledged no God, and a First Amendment that permitted no national church. Foundations were further weakened by icons that did not endure and by iconoclasts who seemingly did, by disestablishments that came abruptly or bitterly, by a decline in theology and in clerical prestige, and by novelty and competition in the religious marketplace that apparently knew no bounds. It was a strange new world for the churches and their much-abused "priests." What odds could be given that it might turn out to be a brave new world as well?

In the half century between the Declaration of Independence and the deaths of Jefferson and Adams, institutional religion in America dramatically changed in size, shape, character, and the relative strength of denominations. In 1776 the two strongest denominations (as measured by territorial dominance) were the Congregationalists and the Episcopalians. A mere fifty years later, the strongest denominations (as measured by number of churches) were the Baptists and the Methodists. Roman Catholics were soon to arrive in great numbers, while simultaneously the frontier would spawn new religious groupings even as it rearranged the loyalties of old ones. But denominational profiles tell only a small part of the story of American religion in a period when all the furniture was being shoved about, all legal structures being revised, all liberty being tested.

CONSTITUTION AND CONSTITUTIONS

Did the Constitution of the United States speak to and for all the people? Technically, yes, since it had indeed won ratification (though not from North Carolina until the end of 1789 and not from Rhode Island until the middle of 1790). But ratification had been a close thing in such pivotal states as Massachusetts, New York, and Virginia, the closeness of the vote indicating much anxiety about a nationalism that would erode or erase all federalism, about a chief executive who might speak with such power that the voice of the people would never be heard. The power elites within the several states had reason to fear for their position and their authority under the new Constitution.

The non–elites had even more to fear. Blacks, whether slave or free, could only deplore the failure of the Constitution to follow through on the implications of the Declaration drawn up eleven years before. The document of 1787 struck false notes with its three-fifths compromise and its temporizing position with respect to the barbaric trade in unfree human beings. As the black abolitionist Sojourner Truth asserted years after ratification, the Constitution, although it looked healthy, had within it an insidious defect. "I take hold of this Constitution and it looks mighty big, and I feel for my rights, but there ain't any there."[1]

Women, black or white, found little comfort in the new frame of government, this despite the stern warning of Abigail Adams to her husband in 1776: "In the new Code of Laws which I suppose it will be necessary for you to make," she wrote, "I desire you would Remember the Ladies, and be more generous and favourable to them than your ancestors. Do not put such unlimited power in the hands of Husbands. Remember all Men would be tyrants if they could."[2] This particular husband responded to his wife, a bit nervously, that he had heard that in the revolutionary age the young people had turned rebellious, "that Indians slighted their guardians and Negroes grew insolent to their Masters," but that until he received Abigail's letter he had entertained no idea whatsoever that "another Tribe more numerous and more powerful than all the rest were grown discontented." John Adams thought or hoped that his wife had just been joking, but she had not, reminding him later that it was a bit ridiculous to talk about peace, goodwill, the emancipation of all nations, and so forth, while "you insist upon retaining an absolute power over Wives." But remember, dearest friend, that all arbitrary power is bound to fall and that we women shall in due time not only "free ourselves" but "subdue our Masters" as well.[3]

With respect to its religious affirmations or assurances, the Constitution pleased hardly anyone. Those who saw themselves as "religious outsiders"[4] found little comfort in a document that gave no explicit guarantee of religious freedom. In some anxiety, therefore, group after group wrote to the nation's first president offering congratulations for his election (on the one hand) but seeking assurances (on the other) that their minority status would not expose them to the tyranny of a religious majority. Newport's Jewish congregation acclaimed the revolutionary ideals of an America that would "give to bigotry no sanction, to persecution no assistance," a happy phrasing that Washington repeated in his comforting reply. To the besieged and harassed knot of Roman Catholics, the President responded with the hope that America would become an example of "justice and liberality" to all the world and that, in particular, this nation would not forget that a Roman Catholic nation had rendered such "important assistance" in the recent War of Independence. These and other assurances Washington offered well before a Bill of Rights had been appended to the Constitution.[5] When in 1791 those amendments were formally ratified, not only did the libertarians Jefferson and Madison applaud, but many more religious folk rejoiced to see the rhetoric of liberty carved into the enduring monuments of law.

Within that amorphous collectivity called "the people," one heard many voices complaining not that the Constitution failed to announce for religious liberty but that it failed to pronounce any abiding and undergirding religious truths. The Constitution affirmed no faith, recognized no church, pledged loyalty to no God, placed itself on no transcendent foundation. Beyond that, however, what little the Constitution did manage to say with respect to religion proved as offensive to this majority as the much that it failed to say. The document of 1787 asserted that "no religious Test shall ever be required as a Qualification to any Office or public Trust under the United States." Any office! Not even the president of the United States would have to be a Protestant, or for that matter a Christian, or for that ultimate matter, a believer in God! Surely this was not only to throw all caution to the wind but the will of the people along with it. In the ratification process in New Hampshire, one spokesman opposed the Constitution on the grounds that "a Turk, a Jew, a Roman Catholic, and what is worse than all, a Universalist, may be President of the United States."[6] Surely, a nation of pietists and Puritans deserved a better fate than that. Despite such sentiments, widely shared as we shall see, the First Congress no less than the framers themselves showed no disposition to use the language of faith or to require its use by those assuming federal office. Such functions and powers were, it seemed, among those "reserved to the States respectively, or to the people."

The states, both before and after the adoption of the federal Constitution, took steps to fill the religious vacuum. State constitutions rang with religious language and proceeded to build on religious assumptions. Though accepting religious liberty as a given of the Revolution, these documents did not accept religious neutrality or indifference as an necessary consequence. They wished to affirm a faith, take a stand, make a statement. In 1776 Delaware by constitutional provision required its public officials to take the following oath: "I do profess faith in God the Father, in Jesus Christ His only Son, and in the Holy Ghost, one God, blessed forevermore; and I do acknowledge the holy scriptures of the Old and New Testament to be given by divine inspiration." Maryland not only required belief in the Christian religion, but beyond that limited its guarantees of religious liberty only to those "persons professing the Christian religion." (For these and other state constitutions, see Appendix B.)

In 1790, well after the drafting of the federal Constitution, the state of Pennsylvania provided that no person would be disqualified from public office on account of his religious sentiments—just as long as he "acknowledges the being of a God, and a future state of rewards and punishments." As late as 1796, Tennessee excluded from office anyone "who denies the being of God, or a future state of rewards and punishments." Tennessee revealed its ambivalence, and that of the country at large, by simultaneously asserting that no religious test "shall ever be required." Clearly, many understood that prohibition to mean that never would any invidious distinction be drawn between Methodist or Baptist, but of course infidels and atheists would never be allowed to hold office.[7]

Several states opted for even greater particularity by requiring that all officeholders be Protestants. This was the position taken by New Jersey in 1776, by Georgia in 1777, by South Carolina in 1778, by Massachusetts in 1780, and by New Hampshire in 1784, the latter reaffirming its position in 1792. By constitutional provision, taxes for the support of Christianity were collected in Maryland, Massachusetts, and New Hampshire long after the Revolution was won and the federal Constitution adopted. Maryland even allowed for the continued support of the Anglican clergy in its midst; Massachusetts invested its legislature with the authority to require all towns "to make suitable provision, at their own expence, for the institution of the public worship of GOD, and for the support and maintenance of public Protestant teachers of piety, religion, and morality." The Bay State legislature also impressed upon its citizens their civic duty of attending church.[8]

If the state and national constitutions took contrary tacks with respect to religion, the tensions within the citizenry could be revealed within a single document. While the Constitutional Convention was busy performing its major task in Philadelphia, the Continental Congress also in 1787 was bringing to completion its extensive deliberations concerning the governance of territory beyond that of the original states. As early as 1780 Congress encouraged the states to surrender their claims to the vast western lands so that, among other things, the federal government would have some source of revenue with which to prosecute the expensive war still under way. By means of much delicate negotiation, land cessions were eventually granted by all those states whose ill-defined western boundaries gave them claims all the way to the Mississippi River. Surveyors could now get to work; settlers could legally stake claims; land could be sold and money collected; but the basic policy question remained: How were these lands (and the people thereon) to be governed? No constitution, either state or federal, applied there, no liberties guaranteed and no responsibilities delineated. The Northwest Ordinance, as the fundamental frame of 1787 came to be called, would shape the character of that region north of the Ohio River and east of the Mississippi—and much else beyond.

Far removed from the centers of civilization and education and religion, these western lands required special nurturing and supervision. Jefferson, who framed the early versions of this ordinance, omitted, as would be expected, any reference to or mention of religion. But Jefferson's draft of 1784 suffered the same fate as his early draft of the Declaration of Independence: namely, it was submitted to a committee, there to be amended, revised, and "improved." In March of 1785 the Congress recommended that the central section of every township be reserved for the support of education, then that the one-mile-square area adjoining it to the north be reserved for the support of religion. Charles Pinckney of South Carolina then proposed that instead of saying "support of religion," the document under discussion should read for the support "of religion and charitable uses." This satisfied some, but not others, who insisted that the word *religion* be dropped altogether. Pinckney then withdrew his amendment. Others proposed language that specified support for charitable purposes, but only New Hampshire, Massachusetts, Virginia, and Delaware voted for this change. All of this parliamentary maneuvering helps to explain otherwise puzzling language in the final version, even as it reveals the fundamental uncertainty or ambivalence of the people with respect to religion and the law, to the church and the state. Just where, and how sharply, ought the lines to be drawn that separate one entity from the other?

At last in July of 1787 the much-debated Northwest Ordinance won the approval of the Continental Congress. Article Three thereof begins as follows: "Religion, Morality and knowledge being necessary to good government and the happiness of mankind, Schools and . . ." Here, like waiting for the next shoe to drop, one expects the next word to be "Churches," so that the main clause would logically and unambiguously read: "Schools and Churches shall forever be encouraged." Who could dispute that if religion and morality were necessary to good government, it followed that churches no less than schools must be encouraged? But as is so often the case, experience wielded more force than logic. And experience, in at least some of the states and among some of the people, was that government should not be in the business of promoting religion, even if religion was necessary to good government and human happiness. Others who thought that government simply had to be in that business, especially in a barbaric and unchurched West, argued for that specially reserved section of land to support the churches. The principle was there, but the votes were not.[9] So the third article in its final form again asserted boldly as its premise, "Religion, Morality and knowledge being necessary to good government and the happiness of mankind," but then concluded more lamely, "schools and the means of education shall forever be encouraged." Just as state constitutions when compared with the federal Constitution revealed great divergence in dealing with religion, so the Northwest Ordinance in a single sentence reflected fundamental differences in both strategy and sentiment.

In interpreting the several constitutions the nation's judiciary revealed their own ambivalence. Early in the nineteenth century, a blasphemer in New York thought he was protected by that state's "no preference" clause. Nonsense, ruled Justice James Kent, for the people need religion and morality "to bind society together." He then added: "The people of this state, in common with the people of this country, profess the general doctrines of Christianity as the rule of their faith and practice." The decision in this case, the justice concluded, rested upon the incontrovertible fact that "we are a Christian people."[10] In Abner Kneeland's even more famous blasphemy case in Massachusetts in the 1830s, the Court similarly concluded that though every form of Christianity could be tolerated, ridicule against that state's religion could not and would not be allowed. In 1817 Pennsylvania upheld Sunday closing laws not on the grounds of rest or recreation but on the solidly Christian grounds that a nonworking Sunday was necessary to keep the people mindful of the future state of rewards and punishments, a reminder necessary to the sanctity of oath taking. A South Carolina Court of Errors, three decades later, observed that in a Christian community "a decent observance" of the Sabbath was to be expected and would be enforced. After all, the court noted, Sunday celebrates the day of resurrection and therefore the victory of life over death.[11] Who could allow such a day to be defiled or ignored?

If the judiciary so often spoke of or assumed a Christian nation, how could the federal Constitution do any less? In the first half of the nineteenth century, many continued to complain not about the Constitution's words but about its silences. The separation of the Constitution from the Christian religion was, exclaimed Congregationalist Samuel Austin, its one "capital defect." Jedidiah Morse, worrying about that provision for "no religious test," argued that the nation without avowedly Christian rulers was doomed. And Congressman Samuel Taggert declared that the omission of Christ from the Constitution was "a national evil of great magnitude."[12] Like Sherlock Holmes's barking dog, the case of the Constitution and religion turned upon its failure to bark, its failure to identify the Christian foundation upon which all else rested.

Later in the nineteenth century, a National Reform Association assumed the task of urging that the Constitution be rewritten in order to pay more respect to "the consciences of the Christian millions" than it seemed to pay to "the INFIDEL FEW." The association proposed that this preamble be inserted before the familiar opening: "Recognizing Almighty God as the source of all authority and power in civil government, and acknowledging the Lord Jesus Christ as the Governor among the nations, His revealed will as the supreme law of the land, in order to constitute a Christian government, we the people . . ."[13] Since a Christian nation with an "atheistic" Constitution was a contradiction in terms, the anomaly must be corrected. For nearly a century members of the National Reform Association labored to make such a correction. Their failure is significant, of course, but so is their effort. For it indicated that the "fathers" with whom we have here been concerned did not speak for all the people any more than the federal Constitution spoke for all the states. Indeed, the early decades of the nineteenth century reveal the churches engaged in a counterrevolution against not just the excesses of French "infidelity" but some aspects of revolutionary thought in America as well.

RELIGIOUS VITALITY AND THE CHURCHES

After all the anti-institutional sentiments and anticlerical diatribes of the *philosophes,* the churches and their clergy in America refused to shrivel up and waste away. The latter, moreover, did not content themselves with some sort of holding action, trying desperately to shore up their *status quo ante bellum.* On the contrary, institutional religion in this period exploded with a new burst of energy, a new breadth of vision, a whole new apparatus for recruitment and expansion. Before the deaths of Jefferson and Adams in 1826, it was obvious to nearly everyone (if not to the patriarchs themselves) that all Americans were not in the process of becoming Unitarians. If explanation be required, the evangelical churches would readily supply it: just as Jesus Christ did not come into the world to save metaphysicians only, neither did he descend from heaven to save *philosophes* only. Even John Adams, at least in his youth, acknowledged the force as well as the necessity of "enthusiasm," that "noble infirmity" without which "no great enterprise for the honor or happiness of mankind" can ever succeed.[14]

The evangelical churches, to adopt both the language and the categories of the early historian Robert Baird, could be subsumed under five broad denominational families: Baptist, Congregational/Presbyterian, Episcopal, Lutheran, and Methodist. These five by midcentury, Baird estimated, had a membership of over four million, with a population of over seventeen million "more or less under the influence of the evangelical denominations."[15] With a national population of around twenty-three million in 1850, America, Baird believed, could still be very much shaped by, if not governed by, the "evangelical mind."[16] Certainly, the churches themselves so believed and so acted in the early decades of the nineteenth century as they accepted all the challenges of new nationhood, new territories, and new circumstances. Chief among the latter was the circumstance of complete and sometimes sudden disestablishment.

To the surprise of many, the elimination of all government support and public taxation on behalf of the churches brought new life, not catastrophe. How this could possibly be true, Lyman Beecher (Congregational clergyman of New England) had first to explain to himself so that he could then explain it to others. As the century opened in Connecticut, Beecher dedicated himself to resisting the efforts of Baptists and Quakers, Episcopalians and Jeffersonian Republicans, to bring about disestablishment in that land of steady habits. Beecher organized, argued, protested, plotted. But the opposition continued its relentless campaign, an opposition that Beecher characterized as including "nearly all the minor sects, besides the Sabbath-breakers, rum-selling tippling folks, infidels, and ruff-scuff generally." Together, this odd lot somehow "overset us. They slung us like a stone from a sling." All this happened in 1818, when by a very close vote of 13,918 to 12,364 Connecticut citizens managed to disestablish the state's Congregational church. Later, Beecher recalled those dark days in Connecticut's history.

It was a time of great depression and suffering. It was the worst attack I ever met in my life, . . . I worked as hard as mortal man could, and at the time preached for revivals with all my might . . . till at last, what with domestic afflictions and all, my health and spirits began to fail. It was as dark a day as ever I saw. The odium thrown upon the ministry was inconceivable. The injury done to the cause of Christ, as we then supposed, was irreparable. For several days I suffered what no tongue can tell *for the best thing that ever happened to the State of Connecticut.* It cut the churches loose from dependence on state support. It threw them wholly on their own resources and on God.[17]

With both wonder and surprise, Beecher felt obliged to report that the result was not loss of churchly influence, but gain.

What historians have come to call the Second Great Awakening gives bountiful evidence that Beecher's observations applied far beyond the borders of that one small state. Against the fears of a godless Constitution and a secular state, contrary to the tendencies of the French Revolution and its infidelity, despite the savagery of the West and its unbridled lawlessness, notwithstanding the fearful unknowns that a heavy non-Protestant immigration promised—against all this and more, the evangelical churches rebounded in the most astonishing and energetic ways. In biblical language that all these churches would not only understand but also regularly use, the fields were white unto harvest and God called his laborers to be faithful stewards in such significant times. To the mighty challenge, the churches and their members responded with new organizations, new denominations, and new techniques.

Much of the new organization sprang out of that novel circumstance of severed connections between civil and ecclesiastical domains. What was called for now was no longer social conformity or political coercion but, on the contrary, an ever-broadening river of voluntary, spontaneous activity. Robert Baird could hardly contain himself in extolling the virtues and the possibilities of what he called the "voluntary principle." This was to be the essence of religion in America and its glory as well. "Adapting itself to every variety of circumstance," Baird wrote, the voluntary principle "acts wherever the Gospel is to be preached, wherever vice is to be attacked, wherever suffering humanity is to be relieved." Of course, voluntarism brought benefit to those who were the objects of its concern, but beyond that, Baird believed that it even benefited those who practiced the principle. "The very activity, energy, and self-reliance it calls forth are great blessings to the individual who exercises these qualities. . . . Men are so constituted as to derive happiness from the cultivation of an independent, energetic, and benevolent spirit, in being co-workers with God."[18] Energy, independence, benevolence—these virtues could bring a kingdom of God to an American earth, even to its westernmost reaches.

Or, if those virtues failed to accomplish that, they at least brought into being organizations and societies that moved powerfully all across that American earth. The spirit of Lyman Beecher lingered on: organize, reform the morals, attack the vice, help the needy, save the world. In 1812 Connecticut saw the creation of a

Society for the Suppression of Vice and Promotion of Good Morals; in 1814 New York's evangelical citizens formed an Association for the Relief of Respectable, Aged, Indigent Females, this to be followed three years later by a Boston Society for the Moral and Religious Instruction of the Poor. Horace Mann reformed education; Timothy Flint denounced gambling; Lyman Beecher attacked dueling; Benjamin Rush promoted temperance; Lucretia Mott fought for the rights of women; William Ellery Channing resisted war; and Angelina Grimké joined with Theodore Weld in a stirring condemnation of slavery. The churches created Bible societies, Sunday schools, publishing and education unions; they organized for peace and missions; they became, in short, as Baird would have it, co-workers with God and their fellow human beings. The age of voluntarism turned into an age of reform—an American Revolution all over again, only this time not in politics but religion. The boundless optimism of Enlightenment captains had passed, undiluted, into the hands of Evangelical troops.

Denominations as such did not lead these movements, but laymen and laywomen moved out onto the battlefronts; these shock troops provided the vision, strength, financial backing, and personnel. Frontier Sunday schools, for example, gave the laity, especially women, the opportunity to render important services where ordained clergy were few or altogether absent. Missions, whether at home or abroad, featured husbands and wives equal in their dedication and their labors, if not always equal (with apologies to Abigail Adams) in their authority. An American Board of Commissioners for Foreign Missions was formed in 1810, this to be followed by an American Home Mission Society in 1826. A host of other denominations soon imitated these basically Congregational entities. Evangelical religion in the nineteenth century girded itself to redeem not only America but the whole world.

More than forest clearing and subsistence farming altered the landscape of the trans-Appalachian West. Baird's evangelical denominations planted colleges in amazing numbers in Tennessee and Kentucky, in Ohio and Illinois, and eventually in another West far beyond the Mississippi River. Prior to the Civil War the denominations established themselves as the controlling force in higher education, naturally enough in all those institutions that they founded but even in those state schools they had not. Denominations determined to maintain a learned clergy would be expected to lead in the creation of colleges, but even those religious bodies not so bound to the notion of an educated ministry proceeded with equal energy (and even on occasion in greater numbers) to bring their schools and colleges into being. It was what Lyman Beecher dreamed of in "his" West, he and his family having moved from New England to Cincinnati in 1832. Just as the sun and rain of heaven call forth a bounteous vegetation, so (Beecher wrote in 1835) will "Bibles, and Sabbaths, and schools, and seminaries . . . diffuse intellectual light and warmth for the bounteous fruits of righteousness and peace."[19] Fresh associations and institutions gave bodily reality to the spiritual visions of a revived and reviving American church.

That "church" found renewed strength in the infusion of new denominational blood. American Methodism was born in 1784, one year after the end of the Revolution and a mere five years before George Washington accepted the nomination for the presidency. Yet, in the early decades of the nineteenth century, Methodists expanded with a sweep and vigor that astonished all observers. As early as 1792 Jedidiah Morse (the nation's first cultural geographer) tried to keep up with the rapidly expanding populations and denominations. The Methodists dismayed him. "Their numbers are so various in different places, at different times, that it would be a matter of no small difficulty to find out their exact numbers."[20] By 1800 Methodists, only sixteen years old as an American church, numbered at least sixty-five thousand; in a single decade that number more than doubled, then doubled once again by 1830; by 1850 the new nation found itself with over half a million Methodists and with far more Methodist churches than those of Congregationalists, Presbyterians, Episcopalians, and Lutherans combined. Methodists not only increased numerically, they exploded spatially. Every time a new post road went in, Methodist circuit riders rode out before the dirt was dry. Properly educated, formally ordained clergymen reaching their western outposts found the Methodists already there, long before.

Black slaves found Methodism congenial, as they did in even larger proportion the Baptist denomination. As the black Methodist bishop, Richard Allen, noted, "the Methodists were the first people that brought glad tidings to the colored people." The gospel that they brought, moreover, was one wholly accessible to the blacks, "for all other denominations preached so high-flown that we were not able to comprehend their doctrine. Sure am I," Allen observed, "that reading sermons will never prove so beneficial to the colored people as spiritual or extempore preaching."[21] By 1816 an African Methodist Episcopal church arose in Philadelphia and, less than a half-dozen years later, the African Methodist Episcopal Zion church was born in New York City. Each black denomination spurted ahead, determined to match the breathless record of the parent church.[22] Though formal black Baptist organization on a national scale came later in the nineteenth century, local Baptist churches, black in both membership and leadership, flourished from a far earlier time, notably in the southeastern quadrant of the United States.[23]

On the western Pennsylvania frontier, a wholly American denomination came into being, this movement eventually taking the name Disciples of Christ. Thomas Jefferson believed in the restoration of primitive Christianity, and so did the founder of this frontier fellowship, Alexander Campbell. Any sense of common cause was improbable, however, since Campbell entertained doubts about neither the divinity of Christ nor the authority of biblical revelation. Like Jefferson, however, Campbell did have some harsh words for institutional Christianity, especially for its tendency to divide into warring sects, to multiply church entities beyond necessity or reason. What Campbell offered as a cure for this mindless multiplicity was a simple fellowship, an undifferentiated discipleship that would reject all separations and divisions and schisms. Men and women would be designated by no other name but "Christian" and their church by no other label than "Disciples." Campbell's vision of a restored and purified primitive or New Testament church merged with the revivalism of Barton Stone and the frontier camp meetings to forge by 1833 a single movement. Despite Campbell's invective against proliferating denominationalism, he failed to cure the ailment; rather, he provided yet another denomination, which would eventually become three. As newcomers on the American scene the Disciples of Christ, like Methodists, sought to make up for lost time, growing rapidly in their home territory along the Ohio River frontier, but also making significant conquests in the well-churched East.

In upstate New York, everything boiled over in the early nineteenth century. The end-of-the-age predictions of William Miller in the 1830s constituted only the most dramatic expression of a millennialism already firmly lodged in the new republic. The victory at Yorktown in 1781 and the favorably concluded Treaty of Paris two years later spawned many a dream of the kingdom of God about to appear. Such events as those of 1781 and 1783 forged a link, Congregationalist David Tappen declared, "a chain which is gradually drawing after it the most glorious consequences to mankind . . . hastening on the accomplishments of the scripture-prophecies relative to the *Millennial State.*"[24] In Rhode Island the Baptist Warren Association in 1784 noted that the Revolution would do more than bring freedom and independence to America: it would "advance the cause of Christ in the world," being one important step "towards bringing the glory of the latter day."[25] Philadelphia's Benjamin Rush, noted for his biblical millennialism, told the American Philosophical Society in 1786 that God might be on the verge of changing "the human moral character into the likeness of God himself." And Princeton's Samuel Stanhope Smith informed Rush that the new nation stood at such a threshold of possibility as to require, perhaps, no "other millennium than the general progress of science, & Civilization."[26] Whether by God's bounty or by human effort, a new age beckoned and emboldened America.

Drawing upon this foundation of cosmic optimism laid down in the closing years of the eighteenth century, William Miller aroused thousands to look for Christ's coming soon: probably in

1843, certainly in 1844. No exotic or fringe movement, the Miller-
ite version of New World destiny pervaded all the evangelical
denominations and enlivened the hopes of mainstream Protestants. When Christ did not appear as foretold, the resulting "Great
Disappointment," instead of weakening denominational life,
added to its panoply such stalwarts as the Seventh-day Adven-
tists. Upstate New York harbored far more than millennial expec-
tations, as other lively manifestations of institutional religion in
America first found expressions there: the Mormons, the Oneida
Community, the Spiritualists all proved the vitality and energy of
American religion, even if all did not win the approval of Robert
Baird.[27]

Some grew wary of, then hostile toward, a sectarianism that—
despite Campbell—showed no signs of diminishing. How could
religion conquer or keep America if it spoke with so many differing and competing voices? And such voices! Mormonism, said
Robert Baird, was the grossest of all delusions. Shakerism, said
Jedidiah Morse, indulged in a kind of worship of God that deserves to be called by some other name. The Oneida experiment,
said all its neighbors, was only a gross indulgence in free love
thinly disguised under a mask of religion. Overwhelmed by the
novelty and energy of the denominations, Thoreau vowed not to
indulge in "doing-good because the profession was overcrowded,"
while Emerson regretted that a sect has become "an elegant incog-
nito to save a man from the necessity of thinking."[28] However one
might react to all that flourished in the name of religion in early
nineteenth century America, one conclusion could not be dodged:
institutional religion had not been buried, probably not even
bruised, by all the Tom Paines and French infidels, nor by all the
caustic critics of imperious "priests" and power-hungry churches.

Bewildered by a diversity that threatened to nullify religion's
cultural authority or credibility, the evangelical denominations
fought back, flexing their muscles and reasserting their presence.
In 1801 Congregationalists and Presbyterians joined in a Plan of
Union that would enable them to respond more effectively to
Beecher's *Plea for the West.* With their farmer-preachers Baptists

achieved on the frontier an omnipresence that rivaled that of the Methodists. Lutherans and other continental Europeans moved out to Ohio and Indiana, down into the Shenandoah Valley and through the Cumberland Gap. And even though Robert Baird, haunted by the specter of an ever-splintering Protestantism, declined to include Campbell's Disciples within his evangelical category, surely he must be amended at that point. The Disciples of Christ were fellow evangelicals, proclaiming a familiar gospel and scattering their New Testament churches all through Ohio, Kentucky, Tennessee, and Missouri.

In the South at the same time, religion had become—as Donald Mathews and others have so effectively shown—almost exclusively an evangelical affair. With a democratic appeal that reached both male and female, both rich and poor, and even, amazingly, both slave and free, this gospel transformed an aristocratic society tied to an established church into an evangelical community inspired by a voluntary one. Mathews explained that even the slave found hope and promise and comfort in biblical preaching as it reached new heights of power—spiritual and extempore, as Richard Allen had noted. The black Virginia preacher John Jasper convinced slaves that they too could be "more than conquerors through Him who loved us and gave himself for us." If God could take a despised Jew and manifest his heavenly power through him, so could that same omnipotent God take a despised slave and manifest his power through him—and indeed through all slaves. Slaves can claim the promise that the first shall be last, and the last first. They can find strength in knowing that the mighty shall be brought low, and the lowly shall be raised high; prisoners shall be set free, and at last, God's glory shall be fully revealed. All who hear and heed this gospel, all classes and conditions of women and men, can through Jesus Christ become more than conquerors.[29]

Such a gospel was regularly proclaimed from the pulpit on Sundays, but with even greater power this gospel found concentrated expression and propagation through the revival. Revivalism was, of course, not an invention of the nineteenth century, but in that time it reached its apogee in technique and systematic defense.

The Second Great Awakening is often represented solely by its revivalism, and though this is an inappropriate simplification, it would be even more inappropriate to dismiss or bypass a device so deliberately aimed at recruitment and expansion. In the North and in the South, in the cities and in the forests, revivalism pressed the options for salvation hereafter and for Christian community here upon all who gathered together. Peter Cartwright (Methodist) would wrestle bears, if that's what it took, to bring to each troubled soul a peace that passed all understanding. Barton Stone (Disciples) would keep a camp meeting going for weeks and weeks, if that's what it took, to see sinners repent and saints rejoice. Charles Finney (Presbyterian) would leave behind his practice of law and his whole way of life, if that's what it took, to break "the power of the world and of sin" over an unrepentant people.

In 1835 Finney published his *Lectures on Revivals of Religion* to demonstrate that sowing a crop and reaping a harvest were just as natural, just as dependent upon the blessing of God, as were sowing the Word and reaping a great harvest of souls. Finney found nothing second-class or crass about "promoting" revivals any more than in "promoting" religion. Those who argued that revivals somehow compromised the sovereignty of God were mouthing mere nonsense. Every rational human being knows that connections exist between means and ends; this truth obtains whether one speaks of reaping grain or reaping souls. "Why, generation after generation have gone down to hell," Finney declaimed, "while the church has been dreaming, and waiting for God to save them without the use of means."[30]

Along with revivalism (and Roman Catholics had their "retreats" in this period as well) came a renewed emphasis on perfectionism. This was more than the utopian call to a few to flee the cities for the mountains, there to create a perfect society in miniature. This newer, broader, more democratic perfectionism spread with powerful effect through much of evangelical Protestantism. Since it moved with power, it inevitably also led to still more denominations being dispersed across the American landscape.

Drawing much inspiration from John Wesley's popular tract *Christian Perfection* as well as from the Bible, perfectionists declared salvation not the goal but only the beginning of the religious life. Receiving God's saving justification was not an occasion for relaxation, only an occasion for pressing on, with disciplined effort, toward God's purifying sanctification. In an earlier era, one might believe that attainment of holiness was restricted to the monks and mystics, the elite and heroic few. Now, one learned that all were called to the earnest contest of becoming holy, of being made perfect "even as your Father in Heaven is perfect." Although the greatest proliferation of holiness and Pentecostal groups is a post–Civil War phenomenon, the first half of the nineteenth century also saw this energizing impulse powerfully released into the bloodstream of the new nation.[31]

In virtually all of this burst of vitality, the fresh associations and techniques, the powerful proclamations of a gospel with universal appeal, the special doctrinal emphases and the intensified church life, the Bible acquired an imposing cultural centrality. Jurists quoted from it, and no courtroom could be without it; presidents (John Quincy Adams, for example) began every day by reading it, or at least began their term of office by taking an oath upon it. Schoolchildren heard it; laws codified it; and morals reflected it. As George Washington and Benjamin Franklin gradually lost their force as icons, the Bible took their place. It became, as Martin Marty has noted, "America's Iconic Book," providing a "protective covering" and investing both private and public life with transcendent meaning.[32] Read for comfort and guidance and sometimes reproof, it could also be read as a key to the puzzles of the cosmos and one's own place therein. And even when not read at all, it remained as a kind of national shrine to be honored by everyone and defamed by none. The creation of the American Bible Society in 1816 may serve as a convenient symbol of the renewed determination that this book be cheaply printed, widely distributed, and powerfully present in American life. Enlightenment critics had blown and blown with all their might against the house of Scripture, but that house had not fallen. In the first

generation of the nineteenth century, far more Americans knew
Moses and Paul than Bacon and Voltaire—and knew them far
better.

Biblical imagery, biblical history, and biblical language pervaded American life to such a degree that a remarkable consensus,
a churchly consensus, prevailed.[33] In that age of voluntarism and
reform, all denominations agreed that the sick should be made
well, the lame should walk, and the blind should have their sight
restored to them. All agreed, early in the century, that ignorance
should be eradicated, war eliminated, and slavery abolished.
Moral reform depended on moral conviction, and—as Jefferson,
Adams, Franklin, Washington, and Madison all observed—morality depended directly on religion. The religion in question drew so
heavily from the Bible as to justify placing that book alongside the
Enlightenment as the two great intellectual founts to which the
new nation returned again and again. If this made for inconsistency and tension in the early nineteenth century, that fact may
help account for some of the tensions felt in the late twentieth.

The biblical fount did not dry up, but the waters acquired a
bitter taste when in the 1830s and 1840s Americans found in their
Bible authority both for the preservation of slavery and for its
abolition. Churches, so recently joined in moral reform, now
found themselves arrayed against each other. Some attacked slavery as the nation's most horrendous moral cancer, while others
defended slavery as either morally neutral or a positive good. The
North could speak only of preserving the Union, but for what
purpose? The South could speak only of state sovereignty, but to
what end? Either slavery was, as Michigan Presbyterians declared
in 1835, "A Sin Before God and man . . . a great moral, political,
physical and social evil [that] ought to be immediately and universally abandoned," or, as South Carolina Presbyterians in that same
year announced, slavery was an institution that accorded "with
the precepts of partriarchs, prophets and apostles . . . compatible
with the most fraternal regard to the best good of those servants
whom God may have committed to our charge."[34] Both the nation
and its churches searched for a middle ground between those hard

alternatives, but found none. In the decades prior to the Civil War, religion in America consequently lost much of its credibility and most of its moral authority.

Biblical appeal and biblical rhetoric persisted, however, sometimes as a rebuke to the nation, sometimes as a buttress. At the height of the antislavery crusades, the Unitarian Theodore Parker excoriated those who, seeking that elusive middle ground, maintained that "the law must be obeyed." Immoral law or unjust law, Parker exploded, must not be obeyed! Every crime against God or humanity can be defended by the morally irresponsible who content themselves with asserting that "the law must be obeyed." And Parker turned to the Bible to validate his point. Consider the case of Judas Iscariot, Parker wrote; his thirty pieces of silver, if we follow the argument noted above,

was as honest a fee as any American commissioner or deputy will ever get for a similar service. How mistaken we are! Judas Iscariot is not a traitor; he was a great patriot; he conquered his prejudices, performed a disagreeable duty . . . he kept the law and the Constitution, and did all that he could to "save the Union"; nay, he was a saint . . . Sancte Iscariot, ora pro nobis![35]

On the other hand, the Presbyterian Frederick Ross found the slavery system to be totally in harmony with the Bible. The problem with the abolitionists, he observed, is that they think Jefferson more inspired by the Holy Spirit than Moses or Paul. The Bible is not an antislavery tract, and "you get nothing by torturing the English version . . . [or] by applying the rack to the Hebrew and Greek." All that the Constitutional radicals and French infidels have succeeded in doing is satisfying the "Southern slave-holder . . . as never before, that the relation of master and slave is sanctioned by the Bible; and he feels, as never before, the obligations of the word of God."[36] Both sides appealed to the same book and prayed to the same God, as Lincoln sorrowfully observed in 1865, "The prayers of both could not be answered—that of neither has been answered fully."

A generation before war erupted, America's most perceptive

foreign visitor came to its shores, examined its institutions, and reflected on its future. In his *Democracy in America* Alexis de Tocqueville wrote: "I do not know whether all Americans have a sincere faith in their religion—for who can search the human heart?—but I am certain that they hold it to be indispensable to the maintenance of republican institutions."[37] In the new nation Tocqueville discovered religion to be somehow essential to the good health and very survival of the republic. His observation of the 1830s did not attract as much attention then as it has a century and a half later, for in that earlier period he announced what amounted to a truism. Of course, religion somehow and of some sort (preferably Protestant and evangelical) was essential to the republic. Defining the somehow was at that very moment being worked out, as revivalism and utopianism, manifest destiny and private piety, struggled to discover and then demonstrate the way and the how. But Tocqueville's basic premise was as unchallenged in that generation as it had been in the earlier generation of the founding fathers.

The Civil War, however, broke more than the back of a united evangelical and moral front. It made the centrality of religion more problematic and its precise relationship with the republic less clear. Following that war, the nation moved from rural Protestantism to urban and industrial pluralism, from political and military innocence to political and military preeminence, from destiny more or less manifest to destiny more or less misted over. Religion, meanwhile, moved from its ready alliances with science, literature, and philosophy to lonelier cultural outposts; it also moved from relative intellectual assurance and institutional harmony to theological uncertainty and ecclesiastical strife. The guidance of the Constitution and of state constitutions faltered, if twentieth-century judicial decisions may be taken as a fair measure. The energy of voluntarism weakened, if twentieth-century membership statistics may be taken as a fair measure. The optimism of the Enlightenment and confidence in the saving power of Reason faded, if twentieth-century searchings of soul, after Auschwitz, may be taken as a fair measure. After all the shaking of cultural foundations, how much help can a consideration of the nation's emergent decades provide? What those decades do reveal is a strong bond between religion and the new nation. But the strength of that bond depended not so much upon the power of the government as upon the faithfulness of the people.

Just before the Civil War, another European in America, Philip Schaff, refused to be dismayed by the political gloom or religious division or cloudy future. In his view, the prospects for American religion were still "glorious." "Out of the mutual conflict of all," he wrote in 1855, "something wholly new will gradually emerge."[38] In the closing years of the second millennium of the Christian era, patience may be wearing thin. This American experiment in religion: How much time does it require, how much time does it have?

7. Epilogue

"The past is another country," L. P. Hartley wrote in 1953, "they do things differently there." Though we can never duplicate the past, we can nonetheless learn from it, history serving more often as gentle instructor than hobbling burden. And though the past is "another country," continuities nonetheless persist—humanity rarely being presented with the option to start all over again.

In reviewing the American past, especially that period from 1776 to 1826, we learn that complexity and tough decision making are not modern diseases but ancient and enduring realities. We also learn that in the realm of religion the opinions of men and women in those days varied widely, even as they do in our own. Some felt most comfortable with a state (such as Massachusetts) continuing to support, protect, and defend the Protestant public teachers of religion and morals. Others believed that the best chance for the churches to remain true to their divine calling came only as they avoided all governmental embrace. Still others argued that church and clergy could never be trusted with power, that when possessed of it they used it to afflict the body, shackle the mind, and corrupt the soul. With respect to the pursuit of spiritual truth, some argued for the efficacy of reason, some for revelation, some for experience (past) and experiment (future), and many for various combinations of these epistemological instruments. Some lived chiefly by authority and tradition; others sought autonomy ("Self-Reliance") and innovation. Some regarded enthusiasm and zeal as religion's inevitable ally; others saw in such "noble infirmities" religion's and humanity's sure collapse.

Was morality so dependent upon religion as to be virtually inseparable from it, perhaps even identical with it? Was religion so essential to the maintenance of social order and communal responsibility as to be in some degree political, whether one approved or not? Was the state capable of total neutrality where values and commitment were concerned, and if so, was such neu-trality desirable? Did the popular religion of the churches at any point connect with the rational religion of the founders? Or was it to be said of America and her many religions, as Gibbon said of the religions of the Roman Empire, the people viewed them as all equally true, the philosophers as all equally false, the magistrates as all equally useful? Finally, was religion in this period essentially individualistic and private ("solely between man and his creator," as Jefferson averred), or was it primarily communal and public (as the very existence of churches on so large a scale suggested)?

Tocqueville, worrying about the emphasis on equality in Amer-ica, saw the possible unhappy consequence that its citizens would indulge in a frantic pursuit of self-interest. Equality, he noted, tended to isolate Americans from each other, "to concentrate every man's attention upon himself; and it lays open the soul to an inordinate love of material gratification." The great advantage that religion brings to a democracy is that it inspires "diametrically opposite principles." All religions, Tocqueville said, hold out ob-jects of desire above and beyond oneself; they raise the soul "far above the region of the senses. Nor is there any which does not impose on man some duties toward his kind, and thus draw him at times from the contemplation of himself." Religion, therefore, moderated the unfortunate extremes of individualism, just as it helped women and men to preserve their freedom in the face of a tyrannical majority or an authoritarian state.[1] Religion offered that firm bit of ground that Archimedes searched for, giving the believer the necessary leverage by which to judge or resist the state.

Ralph Waldo Emerson, on the other hand, did not worry about excessive individualism, but about excessive sacrifice of one's gen-ius and virtue to the leveling and homogenizing of the group. Democracy confused equality with mediocrity, freedom with av-eraging. And "in churches, every healthy and thoughtful mind finds itself . . . checked, cribbed, confined." The Church deserved to survive, Emerson wrote, not when it perpetuated tradition or tried to recapture that which had passed, but only when it con-stantly transformed itself into something new and extemporane-

ous. Either the Church "springs from the sentiment of men, or it
does not exist." Like Franklin and others, Emerson discovered the
purity of both worship and doctrine only in the good works
flowing therefrom. So far as doctrine was concerned, Emerson
thought that the second half of the nineteenth century would
reveal "a more realistic church," one that would trade its "obsti-
nate polemics" for the endeavor "to excel each other in good
works." Like Jefferson and others, Emerson thought that the moral
sentiment "speaks to every man the law after which the Universe
was made." That law must be pursued, with all the miracle mon-
gering and dogma dividing cast aside. "I am glad," Emerson wrote
in 1869, "to hear each sect complain that they do not now hold
the opinions they are charged with."[2]

Between Tocqueville and Emerson the concern for individualism pulled against the concern for community, a tension that
persisted through succeeding generations, a tension that demanded and demands the best of both reflection and resolve.
Though Emerson much admired the founding fathers, he did not
admire the spirit that was content with mere imitation or that was
prepared to trust all to tradition and inertia. Whatever "dangers
and dragons" beset the nation at any time, Emerson observed,
successful struggles against them cannot "be accomplished by
dunces or idlers." "Liberty, like religion, is a short and hasty fruit,
and like all power subsists only by new rallyings on the source of
inspiration."[3]

In the decades after Tocqueville and Emerson, Americans found
themselves caught in the tensions between personal freedom and
public necessity, between the commitment to religious liberty and
the concern for a common morality, between traditional assumptions and unsettling innovations. When tensions turned into con-
flicts, citizens looked to the courts, hoping to find there, if not
inspiration, at least resolution. Every question of right and wrong,
truth and error, wisdom and folly, tended to be treated as a juridi-
cal problem or a constitutional question, a preoccupation (as Justice Frankfurter pointed out) that reduced all values to a single
scale.

Such a preoccupation prevented the kind of search within one's own soul that Emerson encouraged; it also prevented the kind of appropriation of a shared past, including the religious past, to which Tocqueville was so sensitive. The Constitution, nonetheless, had to serve as both the symbol and foundation of unity in a nation torn by slavery, distracted by ethnic and religious diversity, and strained by the opposing forces of national interest on the one hand and private liberty on the other. For much of the nineteenth century, the courts, in interpreting that Constitution, sought to enhance its unifying effect by allying it with the "Christian principles" of the American people. Christianity was "so interwoven with the web and woof" of government that to try to remove it altogether from the public realm was to court moral anarchy and educational disaster.[4] Yet, as the nation became increasingly pluralistic if not secular, the courts (both state and federal) found Jefferson and Madison increasingly useful, increasingly relevant. For a people with a national church, expressed or implied, the libertarianism of those Virginians would miss the mark. But for a nation of growing heterogeneity and rampant secularity, the odd notion that government should simply leave religion alone acquired new force and persuasive power.

After all, the founding fathers had not brought about the Second Great Awakening, nor should they have done so, nor did believers of that day desire that they should do so. Some tasks, some responsibilities, some opportunities remained for the churches and for the people. "Let the mind loose," John Adams wrote; "Almighty God hath made the mind free," Jefferson declared. But it was left then, as now, to the people to determine what free and unfettered minds should do, especially in the realm of religion. Free fellowships of faith, free associations for commitment and loyalty that transcended political structure and purpose—these were the agencies to rally on those new sources of inspiration. What good deed can government do for religion? The best deed of all: leave it free and unencumbered, burdened by neither enmity nor amity.

Do we not, nonetheless, remain (in the often quoted words of

Justice William O. Douglas) "a religious people whose institutions presuppose a Supreme Being"? Perhaps, but one must be cautious about any "therefore" that follows. Justice Douglas was himself quite careful, concerned that his words not be misunderstood or misapplied. When later quoting his 1952 opinion, Justice Douglas immediately added, "If a religious leaven is to be worked into the affairs of our people, it is to be done by individuals and groups, not by the Government."[5] Yes, we are a religious people; no, it does not therefore follow that government must become the enforcer or supporter of this or that or all religion. Some would even argue that the best way to subvert "a religious people" is through the mechanism of government intervention and stamps of approval. Once, when hopes were high and challenges enormous, the voluntary principle demonstrated its mighty power. Though challenges have not diminished, hopes have given way to a foreboding failure of nerve that finds strength in neither God nor ourselves but only in the heavy hands of the state.

That heavy-handedness is painfully evident in the case of *Wallace* v. *Jaffree* arising from Alabama's law providing for "meditation or voluntary prayer" in that state's public schools. In the United States District Court, Chief Judge W. Brevard Hand indicated in 1982 his great impatience with the application of the First Amendment to the states (by way of the Fourteenth). Only Congress had been prohibited from establishing a religion, not the several states. This being true (in Judge Hand's opinion), Alabama could do more than simply pass a law allowing voluntary prayer in the public schools, it could proceed to establish Christianity as the state religion if it so chose. And if this might make some people uncomfortable, well, the Constitution "does not protect people from feeling uncomfortable. A member of a religious minority will have to develop a thicker skin if a state establishment offends him," and this included schoolchildren as well. The U.S. Supreme Court, Hand added, has misread history and "amended the Constitution to the consternation of the republic."[6]

When the case of *Wallace* v. *Jaffree* reached the Supreme Court in 1985, the Alabama law was set aside as constitutionally defective. In a strong dissent, however, Justice Rehnquist sought to dislodge the Jeffersonian-Madisonian tradition, preferring the comfort of governmental favoritism toward all religion. For William Rehnquist, the Jeffersonian "wall" was both bad metaphor and bad history, and Madison's "Memorial and Remonstrance" was irrelevant to the history of the First Amendment.[7] No single national church, to be sure—but many state or national churches posed no problem for the justice.

As Alexis De Tocqueville warned, people shake off their dependence "just long enough to select their master, and then relapse into it again." Two conflicting passions animate us, the Frenchman noted: we want to be led; we wish to remain free. The complexity, if not the absurdity, of our history is revealed in the attempt to satisfy both passions simultaneously. One line of Tocqueville's, Ralph Waldo Emerson would readily endorse: "A nation cannot long remain strong when every man individually belonging to it is weak."[8] Religion, both men believed, gave to the individual a strength that resisted the mindlessness of the mob, the authoritarianism of the state. But to keep such resistance strong, religion had always to be regularly purified and renewed—tasks to which Jefferson and Adams also gave themselves. And the churches of the new nation? Their challenge, in addition to theological renewal, was to call people to that which is beyond and outside themselves, to emphasize mutual obligation and public good, to counter selfishness and pride. Together, churches and people could ensure community and commonweal and commitment. Together, they could also repeatedly and emphatically distinguish between those loyalties due an all-Sovereign God and those due an all-fallible nation.

In the new nation, one found no uniformity of opinion, no ever-present harmony in action. One did find vision and courage and transcendent hope. So great were the possibilities, so imposing the challenges, that every resource of mind, body, and soul was called into service. Neither dunces nor idlers could do much about dangers and dragons in those days, nor—one suspects—in our own.

APPENDIX A

Major Documents Pertinent to Religion
1785–1789

1. JAMES MADISON, "MEMORIAL AND REMONSTRANCE," 1785

[Written when Madison was thirty-four years old, this Virginia document remains the most significant evidence of Madison's thoughts concerning the connection between liberty and religion. Unlike the First Amendment, the "Memorial" was not written by a committee. Also, unlike the First Amendment, this statement did not have to be cut and trimmed to meet the interests of other states, nor did it have to be hurried through in order to get a central government moving. Here, therefore, one sees the deliberate, reflective, informed Madison making a case, not a law, for religious liberty, a case for America to be "an Asylum to the persecuted," a case against all "ecclesiastical establishments."

For alternative versions of the bill put forward by Patrick Henry, see H. J. Eckenrode, *Separation of Church and State in Virginia: A Study in the Development of the Revolution* (Richmond, 1910); and for an informative analysis of all the legislative maneuvering pertaining thereto, see Thomas E. Buckley, S.J., *Church and State in Revolutionary Virginia* (Charlottesville, 1977). The "Memorial" itself is taken from *The Papers of James Madison* (Chicago, 1973), vol. 8, pp. 298–304.]

To the Honorable the General Assembly of the Commonwealth of Virginia
A Memorial and Remonstrance

We the subscribers, citizens of the said Commonwealth, having taken into serious consideration, a Bill printed by order of the last Session of General Assembly, entitled "A Bill establishing a provision for Teachers of the Christian Religion," and conceiving that the same if finally armed with the sanctions of a law, will be a dangerous abuse of power, are bound as faithful members of a free State to remonstrate against it, and to declare the reasons by which we are determined. We remonstrate against the said Bill,

1. Because we hold it for a fundamental and undeniable truth, "that Religion or the duty which we owe to our Creator and the manner of discharging it, can be directed only by reason and conviction, not by force or violence." The Religion then of every man must be left to the conviction and conscience of every man; and it is the right of every man to exercise it as these may dictate. This right is in its nature an unalienable right. It is unalienable, because the opinions of men, depending only on the evidence contemplated by their own minds cannot follow the dictates of other men: It is unalienable also, because what is here a right towards men, is a duty towards the Creator. It is the duty of every man to render to the Creator such homage and such only as he believes to be acceptable to him. This duty is precedent, both in order of time and in degree of obligation, to the claims of Civil Society. Before any man can be considered as a member of Civil Society, he must be considered as a subject of the Governour of the Universe: And if a member of Civil Society, who enters into any subordinate Association, must always do it with a reservation of his duty to the General Authority; much more must every man who becomes a member of any particular Civil Society, do it with a saving of his allegiance to the Universal Sovereign. We maintain therefore that in matters of Religion, no mans right is abridged by the institution of Civil Society and that Religion is wholly exempt from its cognizance. True it is, that no other rule exists, by which

any question which may divide a Society, can be ultimately determined, but the will of the majority; but it is also true that the majority may trespass on the rights of the minority.

2. Because if Religion be exempt from the authority of the Society at large, still less can it be subject to that of the Legislative Body. The latter are but the creatures and vicegerents of the former. Their jurisdiction is both derivative and limited: it is limited with regard to the co-ordinate departments, more necessarily is it limited with regard to the constituents. The preservation of a free Government requires not merely, that the metes and bounds which separate each department of power be invariably maintained; but more especially that neither of them be suffered to overleap the great Barrier which defends the rights of the people. The Rulers who are guilty of such an encroachment, exceed the commission from which they derive their authority, and are Tyrants. The People who submit to it are governed by laws made neither by themselves nor by an authority derived from them, and are slaves.

3. Because it is proper to take alarm at the first experiment on our liberties. We hold this prudent jealousy to be the first duty of Citizens, and one of the noblest characteristics of the late Revolution. The free men of America did not wait till usurped power had strengthened itself by exercise, and entangled the question in precedents. They saw all the consequences in the principle, and they avoided the consequences by denying the principle. We revere this lesson too much soon to forget it. Who does not see that the same authority which can establish Christianity, in exclusion of all other Religions, may establish with the same ease any particular sect of Christians, in exclusion of all other Sects? that the same authority which can force a citizen to contribute three pence only of his property for the support of any one establishment, may force him to conform to any other establishment in all cases whatsoever?

4. Because the Bill violates that equality which ought to be the basis of every law, and which is more indispensible, in proportion as the validity or expediency of any law is more liable to be

impeached. If "all men are by nature equally free and independent," all men are to be considered as entering into Society on equal conditions; as relinquishing no more, and therefore retaining no less, one than another, of their natural rights. Above all are they to be considered as retaining an *'equal* title to the free exercise of Religion according to the dictates of Conscience." Whilst we assert for ourselves a freedom to embrace, to profess and to observe the Religion which we believe to be of divine origin, we cannot deny an equal freedom to those whose minds have not yet yielded to the evidence which has convinced us. If this freedom be abused, it is an offence against God, not against man: To God, therefore, not to man, must an account of it be rendered. As the Bill violates equality by subjecting some to peculiar burdens, so it violates the same principle, by granting to others peculiar exemptions. Are the Quakers and Menonists the only sects who think a compulsive support of their Religions unnecessary and unwarrantable? Can their piety alone be entrusted with the care of public worship? Ought their Religions to be endowed above all others with extraordinary privileges by which proselytes may be enticed from all others? We think too favorably of the justice and good sense of these denominations to believe that they either covet pre-eminences over their fellow citizens or that they will be seduced by them from the common opposition to the measure.

5. Because the Bill implies either that the Civil Magistrate is a competent Judge of Religious Truth; or that he may employ Religion as an engine of Civil policy. The first is an arrogant pretension falsified by the contradictory opinions of Rulers in all ages, and throughout the world: the second an unhallowed perversion of the means of salvation.

6. Because the establishment proposed by the Bill is not requisite for the support of the Christian Religion. To say that it is, is a contradiction to the Christian Religion itself, for every page of it disavows a dependence on the powers of this world: it is a contradiction to fact; for it is known that this Religion both existed and flourished, not only without the support of human laws, but in spite of every opposition from them, and not only during the period of miraculous aid, but long after it had been left to its own evidence and the ordinary care of Providence. Nay, it is a contradiction in terms; for a Religion not invented by human policy, must have pre-existed and been supported, before it was established by human policy. It is moreover to weaken in those who profess this Religion a pious confidence in its innate excellence and the patronage of its Author; and to foster in those who still reject it, a suspicion that its friends are too conscious of its fallacies to trust it to its own merits.

7. Because experience witnesseth that ecclesiastical establishments, instead of maintaining the purity and efficacy of Religion, have had a contrary operation. During almost fifteen centuries has the legal establishment of Christianity been on trial. What have been its fruits? More or less in all places, pride and indolence in the Clergy, ignorance and servility in the laity, in both, superstition, bigotry and persecution. Enquire of the Teachers of Christianity for the ages in which it appeared in its greatest lustre; those of every sect, point to the ages prior to its incorporation with Civil policy. Propose a restoration of this primitive State in which its Teachers depended on the voluntary rewards of their flocks, many of them predict its downfall. On which Side ought their testimony to have greatest weight, when for or when against their interest?

8. Because the establishment in question is not necessary for the support of Civil Government. If it be urged as necessary for the support of Civil Government only as it is a means of supporting Religion, and it be not necessary for the latter purpose, it cannot be necessary for the former. If Religion be not within the cognizance of Civil Government how can its legal establishment be necessary to Civil Government? What influence in fact have ecclesiastical establishments had on Civil Society? In some instances they have been seen to erect a spiritual tyranny on the ruins of the Civil authority; in many instances they have been seen upholding the thrones of political tyranny: in no instance have they been seen the guardians of the liberties of the people. Rulers who wished to subvert the public liberty, may have found an established Clergy convenient auxiliaries. A just Government instituted

to secure & perpetuate it needs them not. Such a Government will be best supported by protecting every Citizen in the enjoyment of his Religion with the same equal hand which protects his person and his property; by neither invading the equal rights of any Sect, nor suffering any Sect to invade those of another.

9. Because the proposed establishment is a departure from that generous policy, which, offering an Asylum to the persecuted and oppressed of every Nation and Religion, promised a lustre to our country, and an accession to the number of its citizens. What a melancholy mark is the Bill of sudden degeneracy? Instead of holding forth an Asylum to the persecuted, it is itself a signal of persecution. It degrades from the equal rank of Citizens all those whose opinions in Religion do not bend to those of the Legislative authority. Distant as it may be in its present form from the Inquisition, it differs from it only in degree. The one is the first step, the other the last in the career of intolerance. The magnanimous sufferer under this cruel scourge in foreign Regions, must view the Bill as a Beacon on our Coast, warning him to seek some other haven, where liberty and philanthropy in their due extent, may offer a more certain repose from his Troubles.

10. Because it will have a like tendency to banish our Citizens. The allurements presented by other situations are every day thinning their number. To superadd a fresh motive to emigration by revoking the liberty which they now enjoy, would be the same species of folly which has dishonoured and depopulated flourishing kingdoms.

11. Because it will destroy that moderation and harmony which the forbearance of our laws to intermeddle with Religion has produced among its several sects. Torrents of blood have been spilt in the old world, by vain attempts of the secular arm, to extinguish Religious discord, by proscribing all difference in Religious opinion. Time has at length revealed the true remedy. Every relaxation of narrow and rigorous policy, wherever it has been tried, has been found to assuage the disease. The American Theatre has exhibited proofs that equal and compleat liberty, if it does not wholly eradicate it, sufficiently destroys its malignant influence on the health

and prosperity of the State. If with the salutary effects of this system under our own eyes, we begin to contract the bounds of Religious freedom, we know no name that will too severely reproach our folly. At least let warning be taken at the first fruits of the threatened innovation. The very appearance of the Bill has transformed "that Christian forbearance, love and charity," which of late mutually prevailed, into animosities and jealousies, which may not soon be appeased. What mischiefs may not be dreaded, should this enemy to the public quiet be armed with the force of a law?

12. Because the policy of the Bill is adverse to the diffusion of the light of Christianity. The first wish of those who enjoy this precious gift ought to be that it may be imparted to the whole race of mankind. Compare the number of those who have as yet received it with the number still remaining under the dominion of false Religions; and how small is the former! Does the policy of the Bill tend to lessen the disproportion? No; it at once discourages those who are strangers to the light of revelation from coming into the Region of it; and countenances by example the nations who continue in darkness, in shutting out those who might convey it to them. Instead of Levelling as far as possible, every obstacle to the victorious progress of Truth, the Bill with an ignoble and unchristian timidity would circumscribe it with a wall of defence against the encroachments of error.

13. Because attempts to enforce by legal sanctions, acts obnoxious to so great a proportion of Citizens, tend to enervate the laws in general, and to slacken the bands of Society. If it be difficult to execute any law which is not generally deemed necessary or salutary, what must be the case, where it is deemed invalid and dangerous? And what may be the effect of so striking an example of impotency in the Government, on its general authority?

14. Because a measure of such singular magnitude and delicacy ought not to be imposed, without the clearest evidence that it is called for by a majority of citizens, and no satisfactory method is yet proposed by which the voice of the majority in this case may be determined, or its influence secured. "The people of the respec-

tive counties are indeed requested to signify their opinion respecting the adoption of the Bill to the next Session of Assembly." But the representation must be made equal, before the voice either of the Representatives or of the Counties will be that of the people. Our hope is that neither of the former will, after due consideration, espouse the dangerous principle of the Bill. Should the event disappoint us, it will still leave us in full confidence, that a fair appeal to the latter will reverse the sentence against our liberties.

15. Because finally, "the equal right of every citizen to the free exercise of his Religion according to the dictates of conscience" is held by the same tenure with all our other rights. If we recur to its origin, it is equally the gift of nature; if we weigh its importance, it cannot be less dear to us; if we consult the "Declaration of those rights which pertain to the good people of Virginia, as the basis and foundation of Government," it is enumerated with equal solemnity, or rather studied emphasis. Either then, we must say, that the Will of the Legislature is the only measure of their authority; and that in the plenitude of this authority, they may sweep away all our fundamental rights; or, that they are bound to leave this particular right untouched and sacred: Either we must say, that they may controul the freedom of the press, may abolish the Trial by Jury, may swallow up the Executive and Judiciary Powers of the State; nay that they may despoil us of our very right of suffrage, and erect themselves into an independent and hereditary Assembly or, we must say, that they have no authority to enact into law the Bill under consideration. We the Subscribers say, that the General Assembly of this Commonwealth have no such authority: And that no effort may be omitted on our part against so dangerous an usurpation, we oppose to it, this remonstrance; earnestly praying, as we are in duty bound, that the Supreme Lawgiver of the Universe, by illuminating those to whom it is addressed, may on the one hand, turn their Councils from every act which would affront his holy prerogative, or violate the trust committed to them: and on the other, guide them into every mea-

sure which may be worthy of his [blessing, may re]dound to their own praise, and may establish more firmly the liberties, the prosperity and the happiness of the Commonwealth.

2. THOMAS JEFFERSON, STATUTE FOR ESTABLISHING RELIGIOUS FREEDOM, 1786

[When sentiment in the Virginia Assembly shifted away from Patrick Henry's Bill Establishing a Provision for Teachers of the Christian Religion in favor of Madison's "Memorial and Remonstrance," the way was finally cleared for the passage of Jefferson's long-delayed bill. Written in 1777 and first introduced into the legislature in 1779, the bill at last became law on January 16, 1786. Jefferson saw this achievement as a major breakthrough not only for Virginia or even for the United States: it set the whole Western world moving toward that day when "the reason of man may be trusted with the formation of his own opinions." Jefferson asked to be remembered for the writing of this Statute and the Declaration of Independence.

Finding his homage to reason too extravagant for their own taste, the Virginia legislators did not pass the bill precisely as Jefferson had written it. For the earlier version, see *The Papers of Thomas Jefferson* (Princeton, 1950), vol 2, 545–47. The Statute, as printed below, is taken from W. W. Hening, ed., *The Statutes at Large* . . . (Richmond, 1823), vol. 12, pp. 84–86.]

An Act for Establishing Religious Freedom

I. Whereas Almighty God hath created the mind free; that all attempts to influence it by temporal punishments or burthens, or by civil incapacitations, tend only to beget habits of hypocrisy and meanness, and are a departure from the plan of the Holy author of our religion, who being Lord both of body and mind, yet chose not to propagate it by coercions on either, as was in his Almighty power to do; that the impious presumption of legislators and rulers, civil as well as ecclesiastical, who being themselves but fallible and uninspired men, have assumed dominion over the faith of others, setting up their own opinions and modes of thinking as the only true and infallible, and as such endeavouring to impose them on others, hath established and maintained false religions over the greatest part of the world, and through all time; that to compel a man to furnish contributions of money for the propagation of opinions which he disbelieves, is sinful and tyrannical; that even the forcing him to support this or that teacher of his own religious persuasion, is depriving him of the comfortable liberty of giving his contributions to the particular pastor, whose morals he would make his pattern, and whose powers he feels most persuasive to righteousness, and is withdrawing from the ministry those temporary rewards, which proceeding from an approbation of their personal conduct, are an additional incitement to earnest and unremitting labours for the instruction of mankind; that our civil rights have no dependence on our religious opinions, any more than our opinions in physics or geometry; that therefore the proscribing any citizen as unworthy the public confidence by laying upon him an incapacity of being called to offices of trust and emolument, unless he profess or renounce this or that religious opinion, is depriving him injuriously of those privileges and advantages to which in common with his fellow-citizens he has a natural right; that it tends only to corrupt the principles of that religion it is meant to encourage, by bribing with a monopoly of wordly honours and emoluments, those who will externally profess and conform to it; that though indeed these are criminal who do not withstand such temptation, yet neither are those innocent who lay the bait in their way; that to suffer the civil magistrate to intrude his powers into the field of opinion, and to restrain the profession or propagation of principles on supposition of their ill tendency, is a dangerous fallacy, which at once destroys all religious liberty, because he being of course judge of that tendency will make his opinions the rule of judgment; and approve or condemn the sentiments of others only as they shall square with or differ from his own; that it is time enough for the rightful purposes of civil government, for its officers to interfere when principles break out into overt acts against peace and good order; and finally, that truth is great and will prevail if left to herself, that she is the proper and sufficient antagonist to error, and has nothing to fear from the conflict, unless by human interposition disarmed of her natural weapons, free argument and debate, errors ceasing to be dangerous when it is permitted freely to contradict them:

II. *Be it enacted by the General Assembly,* That no man shall be compelled to frequent or support any religious worship, place, or ministry whatsoever, nor shall be enforced, restrained, molested, or burthened in his body or goods, nor shall otherwise suffer on account of his religious opinions or belief; but that all men shall be free to profess, and by argument to maintain, their opinion in matters of religion, and that the same shall in no wise diminish, enlarge, or affect their civil capacities.

III. And though we well know that this assembly elected by the people for the ordinary purposes of legislation only, have no power to restrain the acts of succeeding assemblies, constituted with powers equal to our own, and that therefore to declare this act to be irrevocable would be of no effect in law; yet we are free to declare, and do declare, that the rights hereby asserted are of the natural rights of mankind, and that if any act shall be hereafter passed to repeal the present, or to narrow its operation, such act will be an infringement of natural right.

3. NORTHWEST ORDINANCE, 1787: DRAFTS AND PROPOSALS

[In 1784 Thomas Jefferson took the lead in drafting a document that would govern the western territory recently acquired by the United States as a result of its victory in the American Revolution. After committee revisions, Congress passed the Ordinance of 1784 on April 23. Though this document did provide for the abolition of all involuntary servitude after 1800, it did not make any provision for religious liberty and, in fact, mentioned religion not at all.

The more famous and more influential Northwest Ordinance of 1787 (which superseded that of 1784) does, however, treat religion in two aspects: its liberty, and its necessity. The very first of the six "articles of compact" protects the religious liberty of those citizens moving out into the Old Northwest. This article gave members of the Continental Congress no particular difficulty since, by 1787, virtually all states had such protection built into their own respective constitutions (see appendix B). The Third Article, on the other hand, which dealt with religion's necessity, proved to be much more problematic. If religion was necessary in the savage and uncivilized West, then what responsibility did government have for aiding and supporting such religion? That did not prove easy to answer in 1787—or two hundred years later.

The following discussion and drafts are taken from the *Journals of the Continental Congress,* vol. 28, John C. Fitzpatrick, ed., January 11–June 30, 1785 (Washington, 1936); and, vol. 32, Roscoe R. Hill, ed., January 17–July 20, 1787 (Washington, 1936). Also see Julian P. Boyd, ed., *Papers of Thomas Jefferson* (Princeton, 1952), vol. 6, 581–617.]

A. APRIL 23, 1785

The following paragraph in the Ordinance being under debate: "There shall be reserved the central Section of every Township, for the maintenance of public Schools; and the Section immediately adjoining the same to the northward, for the support of religion. The profits arising therefrom in both instances, to be applied for ever according to the will of the majority of male residents of full age within the same." A motion was made by Mr. [Charles] Pinckney, seconded by Mr. [William] Grayson, to amend the paragraph by striking out these words, "for the support of religion"; and in their place to insert, "for religious and charitable uses." On which it was moved by Mr. [William] Ellery, seconded by Mr. [Melancton] Smith, to amend the amendment by striking out the words "religious and," so that it read "for charitable uses."

And on the question, shall the words moved to be struck out of the amendment, stand? the yeas and nays being required by Mr. [Charles] Pinckney,

New Hampshire,			*Delaware,*			
Mr. Foster,	ay	ay	Mr. Vining,	ay	ay	
Long,	ay		Bedford,	ay		
Massachusetts,			*Maryland,*			
Mr. Holten,	ay	ay	Mr. McHenry,	no		
King,	ay		J. Henry,	no	no	
Rhode Island,			Hindman,	ay		
Mr. Ellery,	no	no	*Virginia,*			
Howell,	no		Mr. Monroe,	ay		
Connecticut,			Lee,	ay	ay	
Mr. Johnson,	ay } *		Grayson,	ay		
New York,			*North Carolina,*			
Mr. Smith,	no	div.	Mr. Williamson,	ay	div.	
Haring,	ay		Sitgreaves,	no		
Pennsylvania,			*South Carolina,*			
Mr. Gardner,	ay	ay	Mr. Pinckney,	ay } *		
W. Henry,	ay		*Georgia,*			
			Mr. Houstoun,	ay } *		

*Asterisk indicates single vote only; no quorum present for that state.

So the question was lost, and the words were struck out.

And thereupon, the motion of Mr. [Charles] Pinckney for the amendment was withdrawn.

A motion was then made by Mr. [William] Ellery, seconded by Mr. [Melancton] Smith, to strike out the following words in the foregoing paragraph: "and the section immediately adjoining the same to the northward, for the support of religion, the profits arising therefrom in both instances, to be applied for ever according to the will of the majority of male residents of full age within the same." A division of the motion was called for by Mr. [Rufus] King: And on the question, shall the former part stand? namely, "and the section immediately adjoining the same to the northward, for the support of religion." The yeas and nays being required by Mr. [Melancton] Smith and Mr. [Rufus] King,

New Hampshire,			Delaware,		
Mr. Foster,	ay	ay	Mr. Vining,	ay	ay
Long,	ay		Bedford,	ay	
Massachusetts,			Maryland,		
Mr. Holten,	ay	ay	Mr. McHenry,	no	
King,	ay		J. Henry,	no	no
Rhode Island,			Hindman,	ay	
Mr. Ellery,	no	no	Virginia,		
Howell,	no		Mr. Monroe,	ay	
Connecticut,			Lee,	ay	ay
Mr. Johnson,	ay } *		Grayson,	ay	
New York,			North Carolina,		
Mr. Smith,	no	div.	Mr. Williamson,	ay	div.
Haring,	ay		Sitgreaves,	no	
Pennsylvania,			South Carolina,		
Mr. Gardner,	ay	ay	Mr. Pinckney,	ay } *	
W. Henry,	ay		Georgia,		
			Mr. Houstoun,	ay } *	

So the question was lost, and the words were struck out.

A motion was then made by [Mr. Melancton] Smith to strike out the following words "and the section to religion."

Foster	ay	ay	Vining	ay	ay
Long	ay		Bedford	ay	
Holten	ay	ay	McHenry	no	
King	ay		J. Henry	no	no
Ellery	no	no	Hindman	ay	
Howell	no		Monroe	ay	
Johnson	ay } *		Lee	ay	ay
Smith	no	div.	Grayson	ay	
Haring	ay		Williamson	ay	div.
Gardner	ay	ay	Sitgreaves	no	
W. Henry	ay		Pinckney	ay } *	
			Houstoun	ay } *	

A motion was made by Mr. [William Samuel] Johnson, seconded by Mr. [Rufus] King, farther to amend the paragraph by inserting after the word "Schools," the following words, "And the Sections immediately adjoining the same to the northward, for charitable uses"; so that the paragraph read thus; "There shall be reserved the central Section of every Township, for the maintenance of public Schools; and the section immediately adjoining the same to the northward, for charitable uses."

And on the question to agree to this amendment, the yeas and nays being required by Mr. [William Samuel] Johnson,

New Hampshire,			*Delaware,*			
Mr. Foster,	ay	ay	Mr. Vining,	ay	ay	
Long,	ay		Bedford,	ay		
Massachusetts,			*Maryland,*			
Mr. Holten,	ay	ay	Mr. McHenry,	no		
King,	ay		J. Henry,	no	no	
Rhode Island,			Hindman,	ay		
Mr. Ellery,	no	div.	*Virginia,*			
Howell,	ay		Mr. Monroe,	ay		
Connecticut,			Lee,	ay	ay	
Mr. Johnson,	ay } *		Grayson,	ay		
New York,			*North Carolina,*			
Mr. Smith,	no	no	Mr. Williamson,	ay	div.	
Haring,	no		Sitgreaves,	no		
Pennsylvania,			*South Carolina,*			
Mr. Gardner,	ay	div.	Mr. Pinckney,	ay } *		
W. Henry,	no		*Georgia,*			
			Mr. Houstoun,	ay } *		

So the question was lost.

B. JULY 11, 1787 (FIRST READING)

Article the First. No person demeaning himself in a peaceable and orderly manner shall ever be molested on account of his mode of worship or religious sentiments in the said Territory.

Article the Third. Institutions for the promotion of religion and morality, schools and the means of education shall forever be encouraged, and all persons while young shall be taught some useful Occupation.

C. JULY 13, 1787 (THIRD AND FINAL READING)

Article the First. No person demeaning himself in a peaceable and orderly manner shall ever be molested on account of his mode of worship or religious sentiments in the said territory.

Article the Third. Religion, Morality and knowledge being necessary to good government and the happiness of mankind, Schools and the means of education shall forever be encouraged.

4. FIRST AMENDMENT, 1789: DRAFTS AND PROPOSALS

[Being faithful to the intentions of the founders is never an easy task, and probably an impossible one, for at least two reasons. First, the founders (and now I include the delegates to the Constitutional Convention along with the members of the First Congress) were not all of one intention or one mind; second, to reproduce their intentions precisely, it is necessary to reproduce their world, and this we manifestly cannot do. With respect to the Bill of Rights specifically, a whole set of anxieties surrounded the nation's first senators and representatives: Will the new central government become a new tyranny? Will the states be any safer under an American constitution than they were under a British one? Will North Carolina and Rhode Island ever come in the Union? Will this federal experiment ever get off the ground? As William Lee Miller has written, when the First Congress gradually pulled itself together, the United States government consisted of little else but George Washington and a piece of paper. Much needed to be done in 1789, done quickly and done agreeably.

The authorship of the First Amendment is unknown; it is, almost certainly, collective rather than personal. Since, in order to assure the ratification of the Constitution in Virginia, Madison had pledged to see that a Bill of Rights was added to it, he proceeded in early June of 1789 to do just that, "as I considered myself bound in honor and in duty." The language that emerged at the end of September, however, went through many hands and many alterations. These shifts, insofar as they are known, are indicated below. For the religion phrases themselves, one may be guided by Michael J. Malbin, *Religion and Politics: The Intentions of the Authors of the First Amendment* (Washington, 1978); and by William Lee Miller, *The First Liberty: Religion and the American Republic* (New York, 1986). For the documentation itself, see the series in progress: Linda Grant De Pauw et al., eds., *Documentary History of the First Federal Congress* . . . (Baltimore, 1972 and following).]

A. HOUSE OF REPRESENTATIVES

1) June 7 [1789]. Initial proposals of James Madison. "The Civil Rights of none shall be abridged on account of religious belief or worship, nor shall any national religion be established, nor shall the full and equal rights of conscience be in any manner, nor on any pretext infringed."

   "No state shall violate the equal rights of conscience or the freedom of the press, or the trial by jury in criminal cases."

2) July 28. House Select Committee. "No religion shall be established by law, nor shall the equal rights of conscience be infringed."

3) August 15. Full day of debate with many alterations and additions, with some question, still, whether any such amendment was necessary. Following the suggestion of his own state's ratifying convention, Samuel Livermore of New Hampshire proposed:
   "Congress shall make no laws touching religion, or infringing the rights of conscience."

4) August 20. Fisher Ames (Massachusetts) moved that the following language be adopted by the House, and it was agreed:
   "Congress shall make no law establishing religion, or to prevent the free exercise thereof, or to infringe the rights of conscience."
   [This House version sent to the Senate]

B. SENATE

1) September 3. Several versions passed or rejected in quick succession.

Rejected: "Congress shall not make any law infringing the rights of conscience, or establishing any religious sect or society."

Also rejected: "Congress shall make no law establishing any particular denomination of religion in preference to another, or prohibiting the free exercise thereof, nor shall the rights of conscience be infringed."

Initially rejected, but later passed:

"Congress shall make no law establishing one religious society in preference to others, or to infringe on the rights of conscience."

Passed at the end of the day: "Congress shall make no law establishing religion, or prohibiting the free exercise thereof."

2) September 9.

"Congress shall make no law establishing articles of faith or a mode of worship, or prohibiting the free exercise of religion."

[This Senate version was sent back to the House.]

C. CONFERENCE COMMITTEE

Representatives James Madison (VA), Roger Sherman (CN), and John Vining (DE).

Senators Oliver Ellsworth (CN), Charles Carroll (MD), and William Paterson (NJ).

"Congress shall make no law respecting an establishment of religion, or prohibiting the free exercise thereof."

September 24. Accepted by the House.

September 25. Accepted by the Senate.

Ratified by the States, 1791.

APPENDIX B

Selected State Declarations of Rights and Constitutions with Respect to Religion 1776–1799

[Delegates attending the Constitutional Convention in Philadelphia in 1787, Madison among them, generally agreed that it was best to leave the subject of religion alone. States differed among themselves so much in religious practice and historical tradition that too much attention to the subject would distract, delay, and possibly even scuttle what was an overriding necessity: to have a fundamental frame of government drafted and then ratified. That great variety did in fact exist among the states is amply revealed in the several constitutions adopted or revised during the revolutionary years and shortly after. New England's peculiar pattern is evident, for example, in the sections pertaining to religion from the states of Massachusetts, New Hampshire, and Vermont. The lingering hold of the Anglican establishment can be seen, for example, in the early documents from Maryland and South Carolina. Indeed, at the very time that Jefferson was composing his bill for "Establishing Religious Freedom," working out the implications of the Revolution for religion, Virginia's neighbors to the north and south found little implication—except for a modest measure of toleration.

With respect to religious liberty, how do the state constitutions as a whole compare with the federal Constitution (including the First Amendment)? Do they stand to the left or to the right of the national document? The only possible answer to that last question is "both." On the one hand, many of the states take a more restricted view of religious freedom, limiting officeholders to "Christians" or to adherents of the "Protestant religion." Some states, notably the New England ones, also provide for public support of Protestant "teachers" and for legislative encouragement of attendance upon Protestant worship. On the other hand, many states specifically exclude any and all clergymen from holding any civil office. A protection for conscientious objection to bearing arms is, moreover, written into the constitutions at the state level, but not at the federal. In fact, "conscience" in general receives more local than national assurances.

One other inference to be drawn from the several state constitutions is that religion is no minority or insular affair in the revolutionary and post-revolutionary years. Many historians argue about church membership figures in the colonial period generally and the late eighteenth century particularly. We can never recover them all, but even should we suddenly be presented with accurate data on membership, these remain only modest indicators of the pervasive religious assumptions, the pervading religious ethos. One can scarcely read the professions of faith in the official charters below (see, for example, Pennsylvania, New Hampshire, Tennessee, Delaware) without concluding that religious options were far livelier and more pressing in the time of Adams, Franklin, and Washington than in our own.

All material below is drawn from Francis Newton Thorpe, *The Federal and State Constitutions, Colonial Charters, and Other Organic Laws of the States, Territories, and Colonies,* 7 vols. (Washington, 1909). For further evidence of divisions of opinion within and among the states on what the federal Constitution did or did not say with respect to religion, see Jonathan Elliott, ed., *The Debates in the Several State Conventions on the Adoption of the Federal Constitution,* 5 vols. (Philadelphia, 1876). This old classic is being gradually replaced by the series whose initial volumes were edited by John F. Kaminiski and G. J. Saladino et al., *The Documentary History of the Ratification of the Constitution* (Madison, 1976–).]

1. DELAWARE

A. 1776

Article 22. Every person who shall be chosen a member of either house, or appointed to any office or place of trust . . . shall . . . also make and subscribe the following declaration, to wit:

"I, _____, do profess faith in God the Father, and in Jesus Christ His only Son, and in the Holy Ghost, one God, blessed for evermore; and I do acknowledge the holy scriptures of the Old and New Testament to be given by divine inspiration."

Article 29. There shall be no establishment of any one religious sect in this State in preference to another; and no clergyman or preacher of the gospel, of any denomination, shall be capable of holding any civil office in this State, or of being a member of either of the branches of the legislature, while they continue in the exercise of the pastoral function.

B. 1792

Preamble. . . . Through divine goodness all men have, by nature, the rights of worshipping and serving their Creator according to the dictates of their consciences. . . .

Article I, Section 1. Although it is the duty of all men frequently to assemble together for the public worship of the Author of the universe, and piety and morality, on which the prosperity of communities depends, are thereby promoted; yet no man shall or ought to be compelled to attend any religious worship, to contribute to the erection or support of any place of worship, or to the maintenance of any ministry, against his own free will and consent; and no power shall or ought to be invested in or assumed by any magistrate that shall in any case interfere with, or in any manner control, the rights of conscience, in the free exercise of religious worship, nor a preference be given by law to any religious societies, denominations, or modes of worship.

Article I, Section 2. No religious test shall be required as a qualification to any office, or public trust, under this State.

Article VIII, Section 9. The rights, privileges, immunities, and estates of religious societies and corporate bodies shall remain as if the constitution of this State had not been altered. No clergyman or preacher of the gospel, of any denomination, shall be capable of holding any civil office in this State, or of being a member of either branch of the legislature, while he continues in the exercise of the pastoral or clerical functions.

2. GEORGIA

A. 1777

Article VI. The representatives shall be chosen out of the residents in each county . . . and they shall be of the Protestant religion. . . .

Article LVI. All persons whatever shall have the free exercise of their religion; provided it be not repugnant to the peace and safety of the State; and shall not, unless by consent, support any teacher or teachers except those of their own profession.

Article LXII. No clergyman of any denomination shall be allowed a seat in the legislature.

B. 1789 [PROTESTANT REQUIREMENT DROPPED]

C. 1798

Article IV, Section 10. No person within this State shall, upon any pretence, be deprived of the inestimable privilege of worshipping God in a manner agreeable to his own conscience, nor be compelled to attend any place of worship contrary to his own faith and judgement; nor shall he ever be obliged to pay tithes, taxes, or any other rate, for the building or repairing any place of worship, or for the maintenance of any minister or ministry, contrary to what he believes to be right, or hath voluntarily engaged to do. No one religious society shall ever be established in this State, in preference to another; nor shall any person be denied the enjoyment of any civil right merely on account of his religious principles.

3. KENTUCKY

A. 1792

Article VI, Section 2. . . . Those who conscientiously scruple to bear arms shall not be compelled to do so, but shall pay an equivalent for personal service.

Article XII, Section 3. That all men have a natural and indefeasible right to worship Almighty God according to the dictates of their own consciences; that no man of right can be compelled to attend, erect, or support any place of worship, or to maintain any ministry against his consent; that no human authority can in any case whatever control or interfere with the rights of conscience; and that no preference shall ever be given by law to any religious societies or modes of worship.

Article XII, Section 4. That the civil rights, privileges, or capacities of any citizen shall in no ways be diminished or enlarged on account of his religion.

B. 1799

Article II, Section 26. No person, while he continues to exercise the functions of a clergyman, priest, or teacher of any religious persuasion, society, or sect . . . shall be eligible to the general assembly. . . .

Article VI, Section 1. [Kentucky provided, as did the federal Constitution itself, for officeholders to "affirm" rather than "swear" their oath of office, if conscience so required.]

Article III, Section 28; and Article X, Sections 3 and 4. [Repeat the protections of the 1792 Constitution noted above.]

4. MARYLAND, 1776

Article XXXIII. . . . All persons, professing the Christian religion, are equally entitled to protection in their religious liberty; wherefore no person ought by any law to be molested in his person or estate on account of his religious persuasion or profession, or for his religious practice; unless, under colour of religion, any man shall disturb the good order, peace or safety of the State . . . ; nor ought any person to be compelled to frequent or maintain any particular place of worship, or any particular ministry; yet the Legislature may, in their discretion, lay a general and equal tax, for the support of the Christian religion; leaving to each individual the power of appointing the payment over of the money, collected from him, to the support of any particular place of worship or minister, or for the benefit of the poor of his own denomination, or the poor in general of any particular county; but the churches, chapels, glebes, and all other property now belonging to the Church of England, ought to remain to the Church of England forever.

Article XXXIV. That every gift, sale, or devise of lands, to any minister, public teacher, or preacher of the gospel, as such, or to any religious sect, order or denomination [must have the approval of the Legislature], except always any sale, gift, lease or devise of any quantity of land, not exceeding two acres, for a church, meeting, or their house of worship, and for a burying ground. . . .

Article XXXV. That no other test or qualification ought to be required . . . than such oath of support and fidelity to this State . . . and a declaration of a belief in the Christian religion.

Article XXXVI. That the manner of administering an oath to any person, profession, or denomination, of which such a person is one, generally esteem the most effectual confirmation, by the attestation of the Divine Being. And that the people called Quakers, those called Dunkers, and those called Menonists, holding it unlawful to take oath on any occasion, ought to be allowed to make their solemn affirmation. . . . And further . . . [these dissenters] ought also, on their solemn affirmation, to be admitted as witnesses, in all criminal cases not capital.

5. MASSACHUSETTS, 1780

First Part, Article II. It is the right as well as the duty of all men in society, publicly, and at stated seasons, to worship the SUPREME BEING, the great Creator and Preserver of the universe. And no subject shall be hurt, molested, or restrained, in his person, liberty, or estate, for worshipping GOD in the manner and season most agreeable to the dictates of his own conscience. . . .

Article III. . . . the people of this commonwealth have a right to invest their legislature with power to authorize and require . . . the several towns, parishes, precincts, and other bodies politics, or religious societies, to make suitable provision, at their own expense, for the institution of the public worship of GOD, and for the support and maintenance of public Protestant teachers of piety, religion, and morality, in all cases where such provision shall not be made voluntarily.

And the people of this commonwealth have also a right to . . . enjoin upon all the subjects an attendance upon the instructions of the public teachers aforesaid. . . .

And all moneys paid by the subject to the support of public worship . . . shall, if he require it, be uniformly applied to the support of the public teacher or teachers of his own religious sect or denomination, provided there be any on whose instructions he attends; otherwise it may be paid toward the support of the teacher or teachers of the parish or precinct in which the said moneys are raised.

And every denomination of Christians, demeaning themselves peaceably, and as good subjects of the commonwealth, shall be equally under the protection of the law; and no subordination of any one sect or denomination to another shall ever be established by law.

Second Part, Chapter II, Section 2. The governor shall be chosen annually; and no person shall be eligible to this office, unless

. . . he shall declare himself to be of the Christian religion.

Chapter VI, Article I. [All persons elected to State office or to the Legislature must] make and subscribe the following declaration, viz.: "I, _____, do declare, that I believe the Christian religion, and have firm persuasion of its truth. . . ." [This Article also allows Quakers to "affirm" rather than "swear," but it requires all office-holders to renounce] all allegiance, subjection, and obedience to . . . Great Britain . . . and every other foreign power whatsoever; and that no foreign prince, person, prelate, state, or potentate, hath, or ought to have any jurisdiction, superiority, pre-eminence, authority, dispensing or other power, in any matter, civil, ec-clesiastical, or spiritual within this commonwealth.

6. NEW HAMPSHIRE

A. 1784

Part One, Article I, Section 5. Every individual has a natural and unalienable right to worship GOD according to the dictates of his own conscience, and reason; and no subject shall be hurt, mo-lested, or restrained in his person, liberty or estate for worshipping GOD, in the manner and season most agreeable to the dictates of his own conscience, or for his religious profession, sentiments or persuasion; provided he doth not disturb the public peace, or disturb others, in their religious worship.

Article I, Section 6. As morality and piety, rightly grounded on evangelical principles, will give the best and greatest security to government . . . the people of this state have a right to impower . . . the legislature to authorize from time to time, the several towns, parishes, bodies-corporate, or religious societies within the state, to make adequate provision at their own expence, for the support and maintenance of public protestant teachers of piety, religion and morality. . . . And no portion of any one particular religious sect or denomination, shall ever be compelled to pay towards the support of the teacher or teachers of another persua-sion, sect or denomination.

And every denomination of christians demeaning themselves quietly, and as good subjects of the state, shall be equally under the protection of the law: and no subordination of any one sect or denomination to another, shall ever be established by law.

And nothing herein shall be understood to affect any former contracts made for the support of the ministry; but all such contracts shall remain, and be in the same state as if this constitution had not been made.

Article I, Section 13. No person who is conscientiously scrupulous about the lawfulness of bearing arms, shall be compelled thereto, provided he will pay an equivalent.

Part Two. [Provides that no person be elected governor, senator, representative or member of the Council] who is not of the protestant religion. [Mentioning Quakers specifically, Part Two provides for such persons to take the regular oath of office] omitting the word "swear" and likewise the words "So help me God," subjoined instead thereof, *This I do under the pains and penalties of perjury.*

B. 1792

[In this constitution, all the religious liberties as well as all the religious restrictions of the constitution of 1784 are maintained.]

7. NEW JERSEY, 1776

Article XVIII. That no person shall ever, within this Colony, be deprived of the inestimable privilege of worshipping Almighty God in a manner agreeable to the dictates of his own conscience; nor, under any pretence whatever, be compelled to attend any place of worship, contrary to his own faith and judgment; nor shall any person within this Colony, ever be obliged to pay tithes, taxes, or any other rates, for the purpose of building or repairing any church or churches, place or places of worship, or for the maintenance of any minister or ministry, contrary to what he believes to be right, or has deliberately or voluntarily engaged himself to perform.

Article XIX. That there shall be no establishment of any one

religious sect in this Province, in preference to another: and that
no Protestant inhabitant of this Colony shall be denied the enjoyment of any civil right, merely on account of his religious principles; but that all persons, professing a belief in the faith of any
Protestant sect . . . shall be capable of being elected into any office
of profit or trust, or being a member of either branch of the Legislature.

8. NEW YORK, 1777

Section VIII. [All voters shall] take an oath, or, if of the people
called Quakers, an affirmation, of allegiance to the State.

Article XXXVIII. . . . the free exercise and enjoyment of religious
profession and worship, without discrimination or preference,
shall forever hereafter be allowed, within this State, to all mankind: Provided, that the liberty of conscience, hereby granted,
shall not be so construed as to excuse acts of licentiousness, or
justify practices inconsistent with the peace or safety of this State.

Article XXXIX. . . . no minister of the gospel, or priest of any
denomination whatsoever, shall, at any time hereafter, under any
pretence or description whatever, be eligible to, or capable of
holding, any civil or military office or place within this State.

Article XL. . . . That all such of the inhabitants of this State being
of the people called Quakers as, from scruples of conscience, may
be averse to the bearing of arms, be therefrom excused by the
legislature; and do pay to the State such sums of money, in lieu
of their personal service, as the same may, in the judgment of the
legislature, be worth.

Article XLII. [Renunciation of] all allegiance and subjection to
all and every foreign king, prince, potentate, and State in all matters, ecclesiastical as well as civil.

9. NORTH CAROLINA, 1776

Article XIX. That all men have a natural and unalienable right
to worship Almighty God according to the dictates of their own
consciences.

Article XXXI. That no clergyman, or preacher of the gospel, of any denomination, shall be capable of being a member of either the Senate, House of Commons, or Council of State, while he continues in the exercise of the pastoral function.

Article XXXII. That no person, who shall deny the being of God or the truth of the Protestant religion, or the divine authority either of the Old or New Testaments, or who shall hold religious principles incompatible with the freedom and safety of the State, shall be capable of holding any office or place of trust or profit in the civil department within this State.

Articles XXXIV. That there shall be no establishment of any one religious church or denomination in this State, in preference to any other; neither shall any person, on any pretense whatsoever, be compelled to attend any place of worship contrary to his own faith or judgment, nor be obliged to pay, for the purchase of any glebe, or the building of any house of worship, or for the maintenance of any minister or ministry, contrary to what he believes right, or has voluntarily and personally engaged to perform; but all persons shall be at liberty to exercise their own mode of worship: *Provided,* That nothing herein contained shall be construed to exempt preachers of treasonable or seditious discourses, from legal trial and punishment.

10. PENNSYLVANIA

A. 1776

Declaration of Rights, II. That all men have a natural and un-alienable right to worship Almighty God according to the dictates of their own consciences and understanding: And that no man ought or of right can be compelled to attend any religious worship, or erect or support any place of worship, or maintain any ministry, contrary to, or against, his own free will and consent: Nor can any man, who acknowledges the being of a God, be justly deprived or abridged to any civil right as a citizen, on account of his religious sentiments or peculiar mode of religious worship: And that no authority can or ought to be vested in, or assumed by any power whatever, that shall in any case interfere with, or in any manner control, the right of conscience in the free exercise of religious worship.

Declaration of Rights, VII. . . . Nor can any man who is conscientiously scrupulous of bearing arms, be justly compelled thereto, if he will pay such equivalent. . . .

Frame of Government, Section 10. . . . And each member [of the legislature], before he takes his seat, shall make and subscribe the following declaration, viz:

"I do believe in one God, the creator and governor of the universe, the rewarder to the good and the punisher of the wicked. And I do acknowledge the Scriptures of the Old and New Testament to be given by Divine inspiration."

Frame of Government, Section 45. . . . And all religious societies or bodies of men heretofore united or incorporated for the advancement of religion or learning, or for other pious and charitable purposes, shall be encouraged and protected in the enjoyment of privileges, immunities and estates which they were accustomed to enjoy, or could of right have enjoyed, under the laws and former constitution of this state.

B. 1790

Articles VI, VII, IX. [Reaffirm liberties set down in 1776.]

Article IX, Section 4. That no person, who acknowledges the being of a God, and a future state of rewards and punishments, shall, on account of his religious sentiments, be disqualified to hold any office or place of trust or profit under this commonwealth.

11. SOUTH CAROLINA

A. 1778

Article III. [State officers and privy council to be] all of the Protestant religion.

Article XII. . . . no person shall be eligible to a seat in the said senate unless he be of the Protestant religion.

Article XII. . . . The qualifications of electors shall be that every free white man, and no other person, who acknowledges the being of a God, and believes in the future states of rewards and punishments . . . [shall be eligible to vote]. No person shall be eligible to sit in the house of representative unless he be of the Protestant religion. . . .

Article XXI. . . . no minister of the gospel or public preachers of any religious persuasion, while he continues in the exercise of his pastoral function, and for two years after, shall be eligible either as governor, lieutenant-governor, a member of the senate, house of representatives, or privy council in this State.

Article XXXVIII. That all persons and religious societies who acknowledge that there is one God, and a future state of rewards and punishments, and that God is publicly to be worshipped, shall be freely tolerated. The Christian Protestant religion shall be deemed, and is hereby constituted and declared to be, the established religion of this State. . . . the respective societies of the Church of England that are already formed in this State for the purpose of religious worship, shall still continue incorporate and hold the religious property now in their possession. And that whenever fifteen or more male persons, not under twenty-one years of age, professing the Christian Protestant religion, and agreeing to unite themselves in a society for the purposes of religious worship, they shall (on complying with the terms hereinafter mentioned) be . . . esteemed and regarded in law as of the established religion of the State, and on a petition to the legislature shall be entitled to be incorporated and to enjoy equal privileges. . . . each society so petitioning shall have agreed to and subscribed in a book the following five articles, without which no agreement or union of men upon pretence of religion, shall entitle them to be incorporated and esteemed as a church of the established religion in this State:

1st. That there is one eternal God, and a future state of rewards and punishments.

2d. That God is publicly to be worshipped.

3d. That the Christian religion is the true religion.

4th. That the holy scriptures of the Old and New Testaments are of divine inspiration, and are the rule of faith and practice.

5th. That it is lawful and the duty of every man being thereunto called by those that govern, to bear witness to the truth. . . .

No person shall, by law, be obliged to pay towards the maintenance and support of a religious worship that he does not freely join in, or has not voluntarily engaged to support. But the churches, chapels, parsonages, glebes, and all other property now belonging to any societies of the Church of England, or any other religious societies, shall remain and be secured to them forever.

B. 1790

Article I, Section 23. [Continue prohibition against clergy serving in civil capacities.]

Article VIII, Section 1. The free exercise and enjoyment of religious profession and worship, without discrimination or preference, shall forever hereafter be allowed within this State to all mankind. *Provided,* That the liberty of conscience thereby declared shall not be so construed as to excuse acts of licentiousness, or justify practices inconsistent with the peace or safety of this State.

12. TENNESSEE, 1796

Article VIII, Section 1. . . . no minister of the gospel, or priest of any denomination whatever, shall be eligible to a seat in either house of the legislature.

Article VIII, Section 2. No person who denies the being of God, or a future state of rewards and punishments, shall hold any office in the civil department of this State.

Article XI, Section 3. That all men have a natural and indefeasible right to worship Almighty God according to the dictates of their own consciences; that no man can of right be compelled to attend, erect, or support any place of worship, or to maintain any ministry against his consent; that no human authority can in any case whatever control or interfere with the rights of conscience;

and that no preference shall ever be given by law to any religious establishments or modes of worship.

Article XI, Section 4. That no religious test shall ever be required as a qualification to any office or public trust under this State.

Article XI, Section 28. That no citizen of this State shall be compelled to bear arms, provided he will pay an equivalent, to be ascertained by law.

13. VERMONT

A. 1777

Declaration of Rights, III. That all men have a natural and un-alienable right to worship ALMIGHTY GOD, according to the dictates of their own consciences and understanding, regulated by the word of GOD; and that no man ought, or of right can be compelled to attend any religious worship, or erect, or support any place of worship, or maintain any minister, contrary to the dictates of his conscience; nor can any man who professes the protestant religion, be justly deprived or abridged of any civil right, as a citizen, on account of his religious sentiment, or peculiar mode of worship, and that no authority can . . . interfere with, or in any manner controul, the rights of conscience, in the free exercise of religious worship; nevertheless, every sect or denomination of people ought to observe the Sabbath, or the Lord's day, and keep up, and support, some sort of religious worship, which to them shall seem most agreeable to the revealed will of GOD.

Declaration of Rights, IX. . . . nor can any man who is conscientiously scrupulous of bearing arms, be justly compelled thereto, if he will pay such equivalent. . . .

Frame of Government, Section 9. . . . And each member [of the legislature], before he takes his seat, shall make and subscribe the following declaration, viz.: "I do believe in one God, the Creator and Governor of the universe, the rewarder of the good and punisher of the wicked. And I do acknowledge the scriptures of the old and new testament to be given by divine inspiration, and own and profess the protestant religion."

And no further or other religious test shall ever, hereafter, be required of any civil officer or magistrate in this State.

Frame of Government, Section 41. . . . all religious societies or bodies of men, that have or may be hereafter united and incorporated, for the advancement of religion and learning, or for other pious and charitable purposes, shall be encouraged and protected in the enjoyment of the privileges, immunities and estates which they, in justice, ought to enjoy.

B. 1786

[This Constitution reaffirms the religious provisions of the 1777 document.]

14. VIRGINIA, 1776

Declaration of Rights, Section 16. That religion, or the duty which we owe to our Creator, and the manner of discharging it, can be directed only by reason and conviction, not by force or violence; and therefore all men are equally entitled to the free exercise of religion, according to the dictates of conscience; and that it is the mutual duty of all to practice Christian forbearance, love, and charity towards each other.

[In 1786 the more explicit Jeffersonian statute superseded this declaration; see chapter 3 as well as appendix A above.]

Notes

CHAPTER TWO

1. See Thomas Hughes, S.J., *History of the Society of Jesus in North America, Documents* (New York, 1908), vol. 1, pt. 1, pp. 10 f.
2. In W. S. Perry, ed., *Historical Collections Relating to the American Colonial Church* (New York, reprinted 1969), vol. 4, pp. 11–12.
3. Richard J. Hooker, ed., *The Carolina Backcountry on the Eve of the Revolution* (Chapel Hill, NC, 1953), 100–3.
4. In John C. Van Horne, *Religious Philanthropy and Colonial Slavery* (Urbana, IL, 1985), 112; missionary Joseph Ottolenghe to John Waring, November 19, 1753.
5. Thomas Bradbury Chandler, *An Appeal to the Public, in behalf of the Church of England in America . . .* (New York, 1767), 110 f.
6. J. W. Lydekker, *The Life and Letters of Charles Inglis* (London, 1936), 158–60.
7. In W. S. Perry, ed., *Historical Collections*, vol. 2, pp. 484–85; the words are those of Thomas Barton, the Society's missionary to Lancaster, Pennsylvania.
8. Jonathan Mayhew, *Observations on the Charter and Conduct of the Society for the Propagation of the Gospel* (New York, reprinted 1972), 51–56.
9. In 1750, the approximate numbers of churches in colonial America were as follows: Congregational, 465; Presbyterian, 233 (for a combined total of nearly 700 churches); Anglican, 289; Lutheran, 138; Baptist, 132; German Reformed, 90; Dutch Reformed, 79; Roman Catholic, 30. The number of Quaker meetings was roughly comparable to the number of Lutheran or Baptist churches. See Edwin S. Gaustad, *Historical Atlas of Religion in America* (New York, 1976), app. B.
10. David Lovejoy, *Religious Enthusiasm in the New World* (Cambridge, MA, 1985), 53.
11. Perry Miller, ed., *Roger Williams: His Contribution to the American Tradition* (New York, reprinted 1962), 111.
12. Ibid., 192.
13. Ibid., 162–63.
14. Sydney V. James, *Colonial Rhode Island* (New York, 1975), 70.
15. William Penn, *The Select Works . . .* (London, 1782), vol. 3, pp. 1–2.
16. Ibid., 7–9.
17. Jean R. Soderlund, ed., *William Penn and the Founding of Pennsylvania 1680–1684* (Philadelphia, 1983), 132.
18. Ibid. Penn's legislation did provide for Sunday as a day of rest and worship, his humanitarian concern being expressed in his first draft in these words: "for the ease of man and beast from their common daily labor." But clearly William Penn was no freethinker of the libertine sort, for his laws also provided penalties for "all prizes, stage plays, cards, dice, May games, gamesters,

masques, revels, bull-baitings, cock-fightings, bear-baitings, and the like, which excite the people to rudeness, cruelty, looseness and irreligion." (p. 132, sec. 37).

19. Hughes, *History of the Society of Jesus,* vol. 1, pt. 1, pp. 10 f.

20. Thomas O'Brien Hanley, S.J., *Their Rights & Liberties: The Beginnings of Religious and Political Freedom in Maryland* (Westminister, MD, 1959), 77.

21. Ibid., 115.

22. Reuben Fletcher, *The Lamentable State of New-England* (Boston, 1772), no pagination.

23. Paine as quoted in S. L. Blake, *The Separates or Strict Congregationalists of New-England* (Boston, 1902), 58.

24. 2 Corinthians 6:17.

25. Commissary Roger Price, quoted in H. W. Foote, *Annals of King's Chapel* (Boston, 1896), vol. 1, p. 509.

26. Chandler, *An Appeal,* 114 f.

27. Alvah Hovey, *A Memoir of the Life and Times of the Reverend Isaac Backus* (Boston, 1859), 220 f.

28. Ibid., 210.

29. Robert Middlekauf, *The Glorious Cause: The American Revolution, 1763–1789* (New York, 1982), 48.

30. William Lee Miller, *The First Liberty: Religion and the American Republic* (New York, 1986), 153.

CHAPTER THREE

1. See the delightful and informative study by Adrienne Koch, *Jefferson and Madison: The Great Collaboration* (New York, 1950; reprinted Lanham, Maryland, 1987).

2. Madison to William Bradford, January 24, 1774; William T. Hutchinson and William M. E. Rachal, eds., *The Papers of James Madison* (Chicago, 1962), vol. I, p. 106. Henceforth: Madison, *Papers.*

3. Ibid.

4. Madison to Bradford, April 1, 1774; Madison, *Papers,* vol. I, p. 112.

5. Ibid., 112–13.

6. See George M. Brydon's study in two volumes: *Virginia's Mother Church* (Richmond, 1947; 1952).

7. See the carefully constructed discussion in Thomas E. Buckley, S.J., *Church and State in Revolutionary Virginia, 1776–1787* (Charlottesville, 1977). For the relevant text of Henry's bill, along with many of the legislation petitions, see H. J. Eckenrode, *Separation of Church and State in Virginia* (Richmond, 1910).

8. Buckley, *Church and State* 138–39.

9. See appendix A for this document as well as for the Jefferson Statute passed in 1786.

10. In Dumas Malone, *Jefferson the Virginian* (Boston, 1948), 279.

11. Ibid.

12. Thomas Jefferson, *Notes on the State of Virginia* (New York, 1964; Harper Torchbook edition), 152.

13. Merrill D. Peterson, ed., *The Portable Thomas Jefferson* (New York, 1975), 429.

14. William Lee Miller, *The First Liberty: Religion and the American Republic* (New York, 1986).

15. A. A. Lipscomb and A. E. Bergh, eds., *The Writings of Thomas Jefferson* (Washington, 1907), vol. 11, p. 428.

16. Ibid., vol. 16, p. 281.

17. Dickinson W. Adams, ed., *Jefferson's Extracts from the Gospels,* in *The Papers of Thomas Jefferson,* 2d ser. (Princeton, 1983), 345; to William Baldwin, January 19, 1810.

18. Ibid., 364; to Charles Clay, January 29, 1815.

19. Ibid., 375; to Francis Adrian Van der Kamp, July 30, 1816.

20. Richard Hofstadter and Wilson Smith, eds., *American Higher Education* (Chicago, 1961), vol. 1, p. 175.

21. Adams, ed., *Jefferson's Extracts,* 393; to William Short, April 13, 1820.

22. Ibid.

23. Ibid., 402; to Jared Sparks, November 4, 1820.

24. Ibid., 324; to Moses Robinson, March 23, 1801.

25. Lester J. Cappon, ed., *The Adams-Jefferson Letters* (Chapel Hill, 1959), vol. 2, p. 512; letter dated May 5, 1817.

26. Donald G. Tewksbury, *The Founding of American Colleges and Universities before the Civil War* (New York, 1932), 152.

27. Adams, *Jefferson's Extracts,* 320; to Benjamin Rush, September 23, 1800.

28. See F. L. Hawks, *Contributions to the Ecclesiastical History of the United States of America* (New York, 1836), vol. I, pp. 158–59, 194–95.

29. Saul K. Padover, ed., *The Complete Madison: His Basic Writings* (New York, 1953), 307.

30. Elizabeth Fleet, ed., "Madison's 'Detached Memoranda,'" *William and Mary Quarterly* 3 (October 1946): 554–56.

31. Ibid., 557–58.

32. Ibid., 558.

33. Ibid., 559.

34. Ibid., 560–61.

35. Padover, *Complete Madison,* 308; letter to Edward Livingston, July 10, 1822. Also see Donald L. Drakeman, "Religion and the Republic: James Madison and the First Amendment," *Journal of Church and State,* 25 (Autumn 1983): 33. As Drakeman pointed out, Madison perhaps did not wholly succeed in making his language "absolutely indiscriminate." A portion of the resolution of 1812 (July 9) reads: I recommend "offering fervent supplications that in the present season of calamity and war He would take the American people under His peculiar cause and protection . . . that He would inspire all nations with a love of justice and of accord and with a reverence for the unerring precept of our holy religion to do to others as they would require that others should do to them" (pp. 440–41).

36. Fleet, "Madison's 'Detached Memoranda,'" 560–62.

37. Padover, *Complete Madison,* 309–10; to Robert Walsh, March 2, 1819.

38. Ibid., 309; to Edward Livingston, July 10, 1822.

39. Gaillard Hunt, ed., *The Writings of James Madison* (New York, 1910), vol. 9, pp. 229–31. Beasley's work, published in Philadelphia in 1825, bore the imposing title *A Vindication of the Argument a priori in proof of the Being and Attributes of God, from the Objections of Dr. Waterland.* Madison's tempered reply could not have granted

much solace to his fellow Princetonian (class of 1797).

A major biographer of Madison, Ralph L. Ketcham, in 1960 published "James Madison and Religion—a New Hypothesis," *Journal of Presbyterian History* 38 (June): 65–90. Here Ketcham argued that "Madison's own religious and metaphysical beliefs were more profound and complex than has usually been recognized." Also, "there was an intimate and fruitful relationship between Madison's religious views and sympathies, and the signal contributions he made to the philosophy of religious liberty in a free society" (p. 86). In order to sustain both points, Ketcham must make Madison into more of a theologian than the surviving evidence allows.

Both the Ketcham and the Drakeman articles, along with many other valuable sources, may be found in Robert S. Alley, *James Madison on Religious Liberty* (Buffalo, 1985).

CHAPTER FOUR

1. Hosea 4:1.
2. The Emmons sermon was published in Providence in 1787.
3. 1 Kings 2:2.
4. F. M. Barbour, *A Concordance of the Sayings in Franklin's "Poor Richard"* (Detroit, 1974), 34, 61, 78, 83, 125, 155, 179.
5. Leonard W. Labaree and William B. Wilcox, *Papers of Benjamin Franklin* (New Haven, 1959–1984), vol. 7, pp. 293–95 (December 13, 1757). Henceforth: Franklin, *Papers.*
6. Ibid., vol. 9, pp. 17–19 (January 9, 1760).
7. Ibid., vol. 16, pp. 50–51 (February 23, 1769).
8. See Franklin's letter to Anthony Tissington, January 28, 1772; ibid., vol. 19, pp. 45–46.
9. Ibid., vol. 22, pp. 57–58; to Nathaniel Seidel, June 2, 1775.
10. Ibid., 209–10; September 29, 1775.
11. Quoted in the editor's introduction to Franklin's "Dialogue between Two Presbyterians"; ibid., vol. 2, p. 27; April 10, 1735.
12. Ibid., 30–31.
13. Ibid., vol. 10, pp. 81, 83; Hume's letter to Franklin is dated May 10, 1762, and Franklin's reply May 19 of the same year.
14. Ibid., vol. 9, p. 121; to Mary Stevenson, June 11, 1760.
15. Ibid., vol. 20, p. 289; July 7, 1773.
16. Albert H. Smyth, *Writings of Benjamin Franklin* (New York, 1907), vol. 7, p. 412; to Benjamin Vaughan, November 7, 1779. Henceforth: Franklin, *Writings.*
17. Ibid., vol. 8, p. 154.
18. Franklin B. Dexter, ed., *The Literary Diary of Ezra Stiles* (New York, 1901), vol. 3, p. 387.
19. Ibid.
20. See his "Articles of Belief and Acts of Religion," Franklin, *Papers*, vol. 1, p. 103; November 20, 1728.
21. Franklin advised a young man to choose an older woman for his mistress because (1) their conversation is "more improving and more lastingly agreea-

ble"; (2) when "Women cease to be handsome, they study to be good"; (3) "there is no hazard of Children"; (4) older women are more discreet; (5) one cannot tell the difference between old and young when in the arms of love— "as in the dark all Cats are grey"; (6) it is better to make love to an older woman than debauch a virgin; (7) one may make a young girl miserable, but will only make "an old Woman happy"; and lastly, "They are so grateful!!" See Franklin, *Papers,* vol. 3, pp. 27 ff.; June 25, 1745.

22. Quoted in Dixon Wecter, *The Hero in America* (New York, 1941), 69.
23. Horace W. Smith, *Life and Correspondence of the Rev. William Smith, D. D.* (New York, 1972 [1879]), vol. 2, p. 344.
24. Ibid., 330.
25. Wecter, *Hero in America,* 70.
26. C. C. Sellers, *Benjamin Franklin in Portraiture* (New Haven, 1962), 284–87; plates 17 and 33.
27. Ibid., 195–96; plate 32.
28. Ibid., 401; plate 35.
29. This phrase is found in his "Proposal Relating to the Education of Youth in Pennsylvania" (1749); see Franklin, *Papers,* vol. 3, p. 413.
30. All quotations in this paragraph are taken from the concluding volume of D. S. Freeman's magisterial seven-volume work, *George Washington, A Biography* (New York, 1948–57). The final volume was completed by J. A. Carroll and M. W. Ashworth; see vol. 7, pp. 648–53.
31. See James H. Smylie, "The President as Republican Prophet and King: Clerical Reflections on the Death of Washington," *Journal of Church and State* 18 (Spring 1976): 233–53. Also see Robert P. Hay, "George Washington: American Moses," *American Quarterly* 21 (Winter 1969): 780–91.
32. Garry Wills, *Cincinnatus: George Washington & the Enlightenment* (New York, 1984), 13; for biblical comparisons, see pp. 28–35. Also for a better understanding of Washington's attitude toward and careful exercise of power, see Edmund S. Morgan, *The Genius of George Washington* (New York, 1980).
33. Quoted in Paul F. Boller, Jr., *George Washington and Religion* (Dallas, 1963), 94.
34. Ibid., 97–98; see all of chap. 5.
35. Ibid., 94–96.
36. Ibid., 99.
37. Ibid., 110.
38. Paul F. Boller, Jr., "George Washington and Religious Liberty," *William and Mary Quarterly* 8 (October 1960): 501.
39. Wecter, *Hero in America,* 113.
40. Ibid., 125; see also John C. Fitzpatrick, ed., *The Writings of George Washington* (Washington, 1931–44), vol. 30, p. 291, n. 48.
41. James T. Flexner, *George Washington and the New Nation* (Boston, 1969), 187.
42. Fitzpatrick, ed., *Writings,* vol. 30, p. 293.
43. Ibid., vol. 35, pp. 229–30. As historians have long recognized, much of the language of the Farewell Address is more Hamilton's than Washington's. James Flexner observes (in *George Washington: Anguish and Farewell* [Boston, 1972]) that "Hamilton's Main Draft" of the Address expressed religious sentiments that "Washington had never put down on paper" (p. 300).

Unlike Jefferson and Madison, Hamilton greatly favored the presidential proclamation of days of "fasting humiliation & prayer." "On religious grounds this is very proper—On political, it is very expedient. The Government will be very unwise, if it does not make the most of the religious prepossessions of our people" (Hamilton to James McHenry, undated [late January or early February] 1798; Harold Syrett, ed., *The Papers of Alexander Hamilton,* [New York, 1961–79], vol. 31, p. 345). In the uneasy decade of the 1790s, especially with respect to foreign relations, Hamilton urged the political wisdom of setting the religious ideas of Americans "in active Competition with the Atheistical tenets" of France. "This is an advantage which we shall be very unskilful, if we do not improve to the utmost. And the impulse cannot be too early given. I am persuaded a day of humiliation and prayer besides being very proper would be extremely useful" (to William Smith, April 10, 1797, in Syrett, *Papers,* vol. 21, p. 41). Washington may not have needed any particular encouragement on the matter of presidential proclamations, but clearly if such prompting was required, Hamilton stood ready to provide it. Hamilton's influence over Washington was, of course, a major reason for Jefferson's declining to serve in the cabinet a second term. Washington was no king; Hamilton, nonetheless, was his prime minister.

44. W. C. Wick, *George Washington: An American Icon* (Washington, 1982), 147–49.
45. Ibid., 156–57.
46. Ibid., 166–67.
47. Patricia A. Anderson, *Promoted to Glory: The Apotheosis of George Washington* (Northampton, MA, 1980), 18; also cover.

CHAPTER FIVE

1. To Alexander B. Johnson, February 11, 1823; microfilm edition of *The Adams Papers* (Boston, 1954–57), reel 124. Henceforth: *Adams Papers.*
2. "Dissertation on Canon and Feudal Law," Charles Francis Adams, ed., *The Works of John Adams* (Boston, 1850–56), vol. 3, pp. 447–64; quotation taken from p. 463. Henceforth: C. F. Adams, *Works.*
3. John Adams to Benjamin Waterhouse, October 29, 1805; in Adrienne Koch and William Peden, eds. *The Selected Writings of John and John Quincy Adams* (New York, 1946), 148. But in a letter to John Quincy Adams (November 3, 1815), Adams himself refers to the "Age of Reason" (*Adams Papers,* reel 122).
4. To Thomas Jefferson, July 16, 1814; Lester J. Cappon, ed., *The Adams-Jefferson Letters* (Chapel Hill, 1959), vol. 2, p. 437. Henceforth: Cappon.
5. To Richard Cranch, August 29, 1756; Lyman H. Butterfield, ed., *Adams Family Correspondence* (Cambridge, 1963–73), vol. 1, p. 35. See also the postscript to his letter to Charles Cushing (April 1, 1756) in C. F. Adams, *Works,* vol. 1, pp. 30, 32–35.
6. JA (John Adams) to Samuel Miller, July 8, 1820; C. F. Adams, *Works,* vol. 10, pp. 389–90.
7. JA to John Quincy Adams, November 13, 1816; *Adams Papers,* reel 123.
8. Ibid.
9. JA to Francis Adrian Van der Kemp, January 23, 1813; *Adams Papers,* reel 121.
10. C. F. Adams, *Works,* vol. 3, p. 423 (diary entry for August 14, 1796).
11. JA to Benjamin Rush, February 2, 1807; John A. Schutz and Douglass Adair,

The Spur of Flame: Dialogues of John Adams and Benjamin Rush, 1805–1813 (San Marino, CA, 1966), 160. Henceforth: *Spur of Flame.*

12. JA to Francis Adrian Van der Kemp, Oct. 23, 1816; *Adams Papers,* reel 122. In a letter to John Quincy Adams (November 3, 1815), the father also observed that although Priestley's judgment and reasoning were not always to be envied, his industry and research were admirable; ibid., reel 122.

13. JA to William Smith Shaw, June 16, 1821; *Adams Papers,* reel 124.

14. JA to Alexander B. Johnson, March 24, 1823; *Adams Papers,* reel 124.

15. JA to Horace Holley, July 22, 1818; *Adams Papers,* reel 123.

16. C. F. Adams, *Works,* vol. 3, p. 423 (diary entry for August 14, 1796).

17. JA to Morse, May 19, 1815; *Adams Papers,* reel 122.

18. JA to John Quincy Adams, November 3, 1815; *Adams Papers,* reel 122. On January 3, 1817, John Quincy Adams wrote his father that all his "hopes of a future life" were "founded upon the Gospel of Christ." Nor, he added, would he "cavil or quibble away" what seemed to him clear assertions by Jesus that he was God. "You see my orthodoxy grows upon me." Adrienne Koch and William Peden, eds., *The Selected Writings of John and John Quincy Adams* (New York, 1946), 291–92.

19. JA to Francis Adrian Van der Kemp, November 10, 1815; *Adams Papers,* reel 122. Adams was fond of citing the tolerance of Justin Martyr, contrasting his breadth with the narrowness of the church fathers who followed in the third and fourth centuries. "Justin Martyr," Adams observed, "was as Catholic at least as I am"; to John Quincy Adams, December 19, 1815.

20. JA to Henry Colman, October 28, 1816; *Adams Papers,* reel 122.

21. JA to Louisa Adams (wife of John Quincy Adams), November 11, 1821; *Adams Papers,* reel 124.

22. *Diary and Autobiography of John Adams* (Cambridge, MA, 1961), vol. 1, pp. 41–42; entry for August 14, 1756. Henceforth: *Diary.*

23. JA to Stephen Peabody, November 1, 1815; *Adams Papers,* reel 122.

24. JA to John Quincy Adams, July 24, 1816; *Adams Papers,* reel 122.

25. JA to Elihu Marshall, March 7, 1820; *Adams Papers,* reel 124.

26. JA to Francis Adrian Van der Kemp, May 26, 1816; *Adams Papers,* reel 122.

27. JA to Zabdiel Adams, June 21, 1776; C. F. Adams, *Works,* vol. 10, p. 401.

28. JA to Francis Adrian Van der Kemp, February 23, 1815; *Adams Papers,* reel 122.

29. JA to John Quincy Adams, June 6, 1816; *Adams Papers,* reel 122.

30. Ibid., July 18, 1816.

31. Ibid., July 24, 1816.

32. JA to Benjamin Rush, July 19, 1812; *Spur of Flame,* 239.

33. Ibid. (June 12, 1812), 224. Adams added: "Nothing is more dreaded than the national government meddling with religion. This wild letter, I very much fear, contains seeds of an ecclesiastical history of the U. S. for a century to come."

In 1798 the General Assembly of the Presbyterian church called for a national fast because, in its view, developments in Europe as well as at home threatened the destruction of religion and morals and more besides. "We desire to direct your awakened attention toward that bursting storm which threatens to sweep before it the religious principles, institutions, and morals of our people. We are filled with deep concern and awful dread, whilst we announce it as our conviction that the eternal God has a controversy with our nation and is about to visit us in his sore displeasure" (E. H. Gillett, *History of the Presbyterian Church in the United States of America* [Philadelphia, rev. ed. 1873], vol. 1, pp. 296–97).

John Adams the following March called for a national fast in language that, though not repeating that of the Presbyterians, echoed their sentiments and shared their gloom: As "the most precious interests of the people of the United States are still held in jeopardy by the hostile designs and insidious acts of a foreign nation, as well as by the dissemination among them of those principles, subversive of the foundations of all religious, moral, and social obligations, that have produced incalculable mischief and misery in other countries . . . I have thought proper to recommend . . . that Thursday, the twenty-fifth day of April next [1799], be observed, throughout the United States of America, as a day of solemn humiliation, fasting, and prayer." President Adams's call for repentance that follows sounded much like the Presbyterians' call, and his posture in general was Protestant (if not Presbyterian) specific (C. F. Adams, *Works,* vol. 9, pp. 172–73).

34. JA to Alexander B. Johnson, April 1823; *Adams Papers,* reel 124.
35. JA to Thomas Jefferson, December 8, 1818; Cappon, vol. 2, p. 530.
36. JA to George W. Adams, January 12, 1820; *Adams Papers,* reel 124.
37. JA to Francis Adrian Van der Kemp, January 23, 1813; *Adams Papers,* reel 121.
38. JA to William Plumber, October 27, 1814; *Adams Papers,* reel 122.
39. JA to John Quincy Adams, May 10, 1816; *Adams Papers,* reel 122.
40. JA to Aaron Bancroft, January 24, 1823; *Adams Papers,* reel 124.
41. JA to Stephen Sewall, May 30, 1821; *Adams Papers,* reel 124.
42. Ibid. For similar sentiment, see JA to Joseph Thaxter, August 28, 1822; *Adams Papers,* reel 124.
43. JA to Alexander B. Johnson, March 1, 1823; *Adams Papers,* reel 124.
44. JA to Benjamin Waterhouse, December 19, 1815; *Adams Papers,* reel 122.
45. Ibid.
46. JA to Francis Adrian Van der Kemp, February 12, 1821; *Adams Papers,* reel 124.
47. JA to Peter Stephen Du Ponceau, July 24, 1821; *Adams Papers,* reel 124.
48. JA to Francis Adrian Van der Kemp, February 12, 1821; *Adams Papers,* reel 124. In the years before the American Revolution, however, Adams felt more kindly toward enthusiasm, announcing that "it will be found universally true, that no great enterprise for the honor or happiness of mankind was ever achieved without a large mixture of that noble infirmity"; i.e., enthusiasm. See David S. Lovejoy, *Religious Enthusiasm in the New World: Heresy to Revolution* (Cambridge, MA, 1985), 228.
49. TJ (Thomas Jefferson) to Salma Hale, July 26, 1818; Dickinson W. Adams, ed., *Jefferson's Extracts from the Gospels* (Princeton, 1983), 385. Henceforth: *Extracts.*
50. TJ to Priestley, April 9, 1803; ibid., 328.
51. Ibid.
52. TJ to Edward Dowse, April 19, 1803; ibid., 330. The most popular form of late twentieth century Christianity in America adopts the character of what Jefferson might have called the Hellenic heresy: far more concern for self than for neighbor or the world.
53. TJ to Benjamin Rush, April 21, 1803; ibid., 331–34.
54. TJ to Levi Lincoln, April 26, 1803; ibid., 337–38.
55. TJ to Charles Clay, January 29, 1815; ibid., 363.
56. But see the careful reconstruction in *Extracts,* 55–105.
57. TJ to Francis Adrian Van der Kemp, April 25, 1816; ibid., 369.

58. TJ to Alexander Smyth, January 17, 1825; ibid., 415–16.
59. This concluding sentence represents Jefferson's conflation of Matthew 27:60 with John 19:40. In recounting the parable of the grain of wheat that falls to the ground and dies, thus reproducing life, Jefferson was careful to omit the one verse (John 12:24) that explicitly spoke of eternal life.
60. See Nathan O. Hatch, "The Irony of the Enlightenment . . .," *Journal of the Early Republic* 5 (Summer 1985): 149–75.
61. TJ to JA, April 11, 1823; Cappon, vol. 2, pp. 591–94.
62. TJ to JA, August 15, 1820; ibid., 568.
63. TJ to Ezra Stiles Ely, June 25, 1819; *Extracts*, 387.
64. TJ to Benjamin Waterhouse, July 19, 1822; ibid., 406–7. Athanasius (c. 293–373), important church father and theologian of Alexandria, Egypt, is credited with the triumph of "Nicene Orthodoxy," which included the formal definition of the doctrine of the Trinity: three persons in one essence. Much buffeted in life, Athanasius was not allowed to rest even in death.
65. Ibid.
66. TJ to Timothy Pickering, February 27, 1821; ibid., 403.
67. TJ to Jared Sparks, November 4, 1820; ibid., 401–2.
68. TJ to Timothy Pickering, February 27, 1821; ibid., 403.
69. TJ to James Smith, December 8, 1822; ibid., 409.
70. TJ to Thomas Whittemore, June 5, 1822; ibid., 404.
71. TJ to George Logan, November 12, 1816; ibid., 381.
72. TJ to Margaret Bayard Smith, August 6, 1816; ibid., 376.
73. TJ to Thomas B. Parker, May 15, 1819; ibid., 386.
74. TJ to Charles Clay, December 20, 1814; ibid., 362.
75. TJ to JA, July 5, 1814; Cappon, vol. 2, pp. 432–33.
76. TJ to Salma Hale, July 26, 1818; *Extracts*, 385.
77. TJ to Jared Sparks, November 4, 1820; ibid., 401.
78. TJ to JA, April 11, 1823; ibid., 410.
79. TJ to William Law, June 13, 1814; ibid., 357. See the whole of this important letter (pp. 355–58) for Jefferson's most sustained discussion of the philosophical foundations for ethics.
80. TJ to Isaac Story, December 5, 1801; ibid., 326.
81. TJ to JA, March 14, 1820; Cappon, vol. 2, p. 562.
82. TJ to Benjamin Rush, April 21, 1803; *Extracts*, 334.
83. TJ to JA, January 20, 1821; Cappon, vol. 2, p. 570. Also see Adams's response (February 3, 1821), ibid., vol. 2, p. 571.
84. JA to TJ, May 1, 1812; ibid., vol. 2, p. 301.
85. TJ to Charles Thomson, January 9, 1816; *Extracts*, 365.
86. TJ to Ezra Stiles Ely, June 25, 1819; ibid., 387.
87. TJ to Margaret Bayard Smith, Aug. 6, 1816; ibid., 376.
88. JA to TJ, Sept. 14, 1813; Cappon, vol. 2, pp. 373–74.
89. Ibid.

CHAPTER SIX

1. See her *Narrative* published in Battle Creek, MI in 1878; pp. 146 f.
2. L. H. Butterfield et al., eds. *The Book of Abigail and John: Selected Letters of the Adams Family, 1762–1784* (Cambridge, MA, 1975), 121.

3. Ibid., 123, 127.
4. See the fine book by R. Laurence Moore, *Religious Outsiders and the Making of Americans* (New York, 1986).
5. See Paul F. Boller, Jr., "George Washington and Religious Liberty," *William and Mary Quarterly* 8 (October 1960): 486–506, esp. 502 f.
6. Quoted in Morton Borden, *Jews, Turks, and Infidels* (Chapel Hill, NC, 1984), 16. An anonymous writer to the New York *Daily Advertiser* carefully explained that since the Constitution even permitted a Jew to be elected President "our dear posterity may be ordered to rebuild Jerusalem." Quoted ibid.
7. See Francis Thorpe, *The Federal and State Constitutions*, 7 vols. (Washington, DC, 1909); also see app. B.
8. See app. B.
9. See Jay A. Barrett, *Evolution of the Ordinance of 1787* (New York, 1891); and, John M. Merriam, "The Legislative History of the Ordinance of 1787," *Proceedings of the American Antiquarian Society* 5(1887–88):303–47. Also see app. A.
10. *The People* v. *Ruggles* (1811), cited in H. Frank Way, "The Death of the Christian Nation: The Judiciary and Church-State Relations," *Journal of Church and State* 29.3 (Autumn 1987): 509-29.
11. See Leonard W. Levy, *Blasphemy in Massachusetts: Freedom of Conscience and the Abner Kneeland Case* (New York, 1973). The Pennsylvania and South Carolina cases (*Commonwealth* v. *Wolf*, and *City of Charleston* v. *Ambs*) are cited in the Way study noted ibid., notes 13 and 14.
12. Quoted in Borden, *Jews, Turks, Infidels*, 59.
13. Ibid., 60, 63 f.
14. Quoted in Lovejoy, *Religious Enthusiasm in the New World*, 228.
15. Robert Baird, *Religion in America* (New York, 1856), 532.
16. The phrase is Perry Miller's in his posthumous publication *The Life of the Mind in America: From the Revolution to the Civil War* (New York, 1965).
17. Barbara M. Cross, ed., *The Autobiography of Lyman Beecher* (Cambridge, MA, 1961), vol. 1, pp. 251–53.
18. Baird, *Religion in America*, 365–67.
19. Lyman Beecher, *A Plea for the West* (Cincinnati, 1835), 37–38. On the denominational colleges in this period, see Donald G. Tewksbury, *The Founding of American Colleges and Universities Before the Civil War* (New York, 1932).
20. Jedidiah Morse, *The American Geography*, 2d ed. (London, 1792), 269.
21. *The Life Experience and Gospel Labors of the Rt. Rev. Richard Allen* (New York, 1960 [1793]), 28–30.
22. Edwin S. Gaustad, *Historical Atlas of Religion in America* (New York, 1976), 79–80. In 1850, the following states had more Methodist churches than churches of any other denomination: Ohio (1,529), New York (1,231), Virginia (1,025), Pennsylvania (889), Tennessee (861), Indiana (778), North Carolina (784), South Carolina (484), Maryland (479), Mississippi (454), Illinois (405), New Jersey (312), Texas (176), Arkansas (168), Louisiana (125), Michigan (119), Wisconsin (110), Delaware (106), Florida (87), and Iowa (71). This constituted an amazing edge in well over half the states of the Union.
23. On the efforts of black Baptists to overcome their localism and achieve greater national cooperation, see James M. Washington's *Frustrated Fellowship* (Macon, GA, 1986).
24. Ruth Bloch, *Visionary Republic: Millennial Themes in American Thought* (New York, 1985), 94.

25. Ibid., 101.
26. Ibid., 104.
27. On these and other new actors moving onto the denominational scene, consult Moore, *Religious Outsiders and the Making of Americans.*
28. On Thoreau, see Cushing Strout, *The New Heavens and New Earth: Political Religion in America* (New York, 1974), 120. On Emerson, see Bliss Perry, ed., *The Heart of Emerson's Journals* (Boston, 1926), 49 (in "Self-Reliance" Emerson observed: "If I know your sect, I anticipate your argument"). Baird's comments are in his *Religion in America* (see n. 15), 577–79, and Morse's are in his *American Geography* (see n. 20), 270.
29. See all of Donald Mathews's excellent book, *Religion in the Old South* (Chicago, 1977), but esp. chap. 5; also see Rhys Isaac, *The Transformation of Virginia, 1740–1790* (Chapel Hill, NC, 1982).
30. William G. McLoughlin, ed. *Lectures on Revivals of Religion . . .* (Cambridge, MA, 1960), 14.
31. See Timothy L. Smith, *Revivalism and Social Reform* (New York, 1957). Wesley's *A Plain Account of Christian Perfection* was first published in 1739, revised and reprinted through 1777, then ceaselessly reprinted thereafter.
32. Martin E. Marty's lecture on this subject may be found in Gene M. Tucker and Douglas A. Knight, eds., *Humanizing America's Iconic Book* (Chico, CA, 1982).
33. See Edwin S. Gaustad, "Consensus in America: The Churches' Changing Role," *Journal of Bible and Religion* 36 (March 1968):28–40.
34. *New York Evangelist,* November 21, 1835. C. C. Goen's *Broken Churches, Broken Nation* (Macon, GA, 1986) explicates this episode in illuminating fashion.
35. Quoted in James T. Johnson, ed., *The Bible in American Law, Politics, and Political Rhetoric* (Philadelphia, 1985), 66–67. This entire volume is relevant to the subject under discussion, but especially the first three chapters, "Historical Perspectives."
36. Frederick A. Ross, *Slavery Ordained of God* (Philadelphia, 1857), 98–102.
37. Alexis De Tocqueville, *Democracy in America* (New York, 1966), vol. 1, pp. 305–6.
38. Philip Schaff, *America: A Sketch of Its Political, Social and Religious Character* (Cambridge, MA, 1961 [1855]), 80–81.

CHAPTER SEVEN

1. Tocqueville, *Democracy in America,* pt. 2, bl. 1, chap. 17.
2. R. W. Emerson, *Miscellanies* (Boston, 1878); address to "The Free Religious Association," 381–84, 387–92.
3. Ibid., "The Fortunes of the Republic," 418, 420.
4. H. Frank Way, "The Death of the Christian Nation . . . ," *Journal of Church and State* 29:3 (Autumn 1987): 509–29.
5. Douglas's "religious people" sentence is from *Zorach* v. *Clauson* (1952), the case that found in favor of a New York practice of "dismissed time" during which public school students could receive sectarian instruction off the school grounds. Justice Douglas quoted himself first in a dissenting opinion in *McGowan* v. *Maryland* (1960), then in a concurring opinion in *Engel* v. *Vitale* (1962).
6. 554 Fed.Supp. 1118, 1128.

7. 105 S.Ct. 2508 f.
8. See the concluding chapters of *Democracy in America,* pt. 2, bk. 4, chaps. 56, 57. Tocqueville's communitarian concern informs a recent volume that takes its title from him: Robert N. Bellah et al., *Habits of the Heart: Individualism and Commitment in American Life* (Berkeley, 1985). As is evident in the title, that concern also inspired A. James Reichley's study, *Religion in American Public Life* (Washington, 1985). Though Reichley's review is generally a balanced one, he is more interested in describing how friendly the founders were to religion than in calling attention to their anxiety about too much coziness between the civil and ecclesiastical powers.

Bibliographical Note

For the religious context during the fifty years from 1776 to 1826, one may profitably consult such surveys as Sydney E. Ahlstrom, *A Religious History of the American People* (New Haven: Yale University Press, 1972); Winthrop S. Hudson, *Religion in America* (New York: Scribner, 1965, 1973, 1981; Macmillan, 1986); Robert T. Handy, *A History of the Churches in the United States and Canada* (New York: Oxford University Press, 1977); and Martin E. Marty, *Pilgrims in Their Own Land* (Boston: Little, Brown, 1984). Useful specialized studies examining religion in this half century include Catherine L. Albanese, *Sons of the Fathers: The Civil Religion of the American Revolution* (Philadelphia: Temple University Press, 1976); Sidney E. Mead, *The Old Religion in the Brave New World* (Berkeley and Los Angeles: University of California Press, 1977); Harry S. Stout, *The New England Soul* (New York: Oxford University Press, 1986); and an excellent overview of "Religion, Society, and Politics in Colonial America," *Under the Cope of Heaven* (New York: Oxford University Press, 1986) by Patricia U. Bonomi.

The five founding fathers featured in this study were prolific writers, especially in private and public correspondence. They have all enjoyed (or are enjoying) modern critical editions of their works, ensuring the accuracy of the texts as well as the diligence of the search for all relevant materials. Julian Boyd set the pattern in the First Series of *The Papers of Thomas Jefferson,* with twenty-one volumes published by Princeton University Press 1950–82. A Second Series has now been launched that will carry forward from the year 1791. Dumas Malone's lifework was the six-volume biography *Jefferson and His Time,* the first volume appearing in 1948 and the final one in 1981 (Boston: Little, Brown). In 1986, under the editorship of Merrill Peterson, Macmillan published *Thomas Jefferson: A Reference Biography.*

The publication of *The Papers of Benjamin Franklin* began in 1959 under the editorship of Leonard W. Labaree (New Haven: Yale University Press). Twenty-eight volumes have appeared as of this writing, carrying the Franklin career through 1779 (he died in 1790). Franklin's ever-popular autobiography has gone through countless editions, the latest being a useful critical one edited by J. A. Leo Lemay and P. M. Zall (New York: W. W. Norton, 1986). The latest biography of Franklin is by the British scholar Esmond Wright, *Franklin of Philadelphia* (Cambridge: Harvard University Press, 1986).

William T. Hutchinson launched the publication of the *Papers of James Madison* in 1962, the first ten volumes being issued by the University of Chicago Press (1962-77). Then Robert A. Rutland and Charles F. Hobson assumed the editorial responsibilities, with the University of Virginia Press as publisher of volumes 11-17 (1979-1989). The same press began the Presidential Series in 1984 and the Secretary of State Series in 1986. Irving Brant devoted his career to the study of Madison, the result being six volumes published over a twenty-year period, 1941-1961 (Indianapolis: Bobbs-Merrill). Those six volumes were then condensed into one: *The Fourth President*, issued by the same publisher in 1971. In that same year Ralph Ketcham's valuable study appeared: *James Madison: A Biography* (New York: Macmillan, 1971). When the Madison building of the Library of Congress was formally dedicated in 1980, an exhibition related to the Madisonian career resulted in a handsome work edited by Robert A. Rutland, *James Madison and the Search for Nationhood* (Washington, DC: Library of Congress, 1981).

The Adams Papers, the most ambitious publishing project of all, extends far beyond the life and times of John Adams to succeeding generations of the family. Publications pertinent to the progenitor, all published by Harvard University Press, include the *Diary and Autobiography of John Adams*, edited by Lyman H. Butterfield in four volumes (1961); the *Adams Family Correspondence* in two volumes under the same editorship (1963); Robert J. Taylor, ed., *Papers of John Adams* in six volumes (1977-83); and, now under the general editorship of Richard A. Ryerson, volumes 7 and 8 in 1989. The most recent biography of Adams is that of John Ferling, *John Adams: A Life* (Knoxville: University of Tennessee Press, 1992).

For a great many years, scholars and researchers have waited for a modern critical edition of the papers of George Washington. Patience is now rewarded with the appearance of the initial volumes in an entirely new enterprise. Under the general editorship of W. W. Abbot and with the support of the University of Virginia Press, four volumes of the Colonial Series of *The Papers of George Washington* appeared between 1982 and 1984; three volumes of the Revolutionary War Series (beginning in 1985); three volumes of the Presidential Series (beginning in 1987); two volumes of the Confederation Series (beginning in 1992); and a single volume in 1981, *The Journal of the Proceedings of the President 1793-1797*. James T. Flexner's impressive four-volume study, *George Washington: A Biography* (New York: Scribner's, 1965-1972), has been effectively summarized in a single volume: *Washington, The Indispensable Man* (Boston: Little, Brown, 1974). The latest biography of Washington gives special attention to his qualities as hero and symbol: *George Washington* (New York: Free Press, 1987), but also see Garry Wills, *Cincinnatus: George Washington and the Enlightenment* (Garden City, NY: Doubleday and Co., 1984).

Many recent books probe the relationship between constitutional guarantees and religious expression. Twentieth-century concerns inform if they do not inspire all of the following: William Lee Miller, *The First Liberty: Religion and the American Republic* (New York: Alfred Knopf, 1986); A. James Reichley, *Religion in American Public Life* (Washington, DC: The Brookings Institution, 1985); Thomas J. Curry, *The First Freedoms: Church and State in America to the Passage of the First Amendment* (New York: Oxford University Press, 1986); Christopher F. Mooney, *Public Virtue: Law and the Social Character of Religion* (Notre Dame: University of Notre Dame Press, 1986); David A. Richards, *Toleration and the Constitution* (New York: Oxford University Press, 1986); and three volumes all published by Macmillan and Company—Leonard W. Levy, *The Establishment Clause: Religion and the First Amendment* (1986); Richard P. McBrien, *Caesar's Coin: Religion and Politics in America* (1987); and John T.

Noonan, Jr., *The Believer and the Powers That Are* (1987). Excellent bibliographical guidance through the church-state thicket is offered in the two-volume work edited by John F. Wilson, *Church and State in America* (Westport, CN: Greenwood Press, 1986, 1987).

For superb background on this fifty-year period in American history, see Gordon S. Wood, *Creation of the American Republic* (Chapel Hill, NC: University of North Carolina Press, 1969) as well as his more recent study, *Radicalism and the American Revolution* (Alfred Knopf, 1992); and Michael G. Kammen, *A Machine That Would Go of Itself: The Constitution in American Culture* (Alfred Knopf, 1986) along with his documentary history, *The Origins of the Constitution* (Penguin Books, 1986).

Index